# SUPER PLAYER

DESIGNERBOOKS

# CONTENT

**大久保博人**    Japan    5-47

INSTINCTOY was founded in 2005 by designer  (HIROTO OHKUBO) and began selling figures and toys for spindle. With the successful launch of the terrible/cute unique world design, he began to publish numerous unique design characters. With this character, which describes his story, continues to carry on.

**Roar with Lukas**    Austria    48-59
Character Design, Toy Design , Illustration

**Shelterbank**    Japan    60-69

Shelterbank was found in 2003 based in Nagoya, Japandesigned by solo artist "Yow".  His work includes character designs, apparel designs,paints, ornaments, toys and more.He makes many companies and collaboration. His main work in toy's collaboratedwith production office "HEAD LOCK STUDIO"released in the world range and renowned as crazy,charming, weird and funky characters.His mission is to deliver a big wave of HAPPINESS,EXCITEMENT, and JOY and hang everybody's heartall over the world.

**SHON SIDE**    Taiwan, China    70-73

Toys design, graffiti, illustration and painting are all SHON's favorite and also his strength.
Most of his inspirations are coming from normal life and usual stuff but he always can find a new expressing way to show his ideas.CAP DUCK is the most famous character he creates in these few years.
By combining CAP DUCK with other famous images or pictures, SHON convey his thoughts to the viewers more touchingly and humorously.

**Billy Mac Donald**    Ireland    74-77

Billy Mac Donald is a Designer / Maker based in Dublin, Ireland.
His concentration is on creating objects and images with the aim of disrupting the flow of daily life. By uprooting the primitive, vulgar and unconscious, he aims to uncover a life less rational.

**Jeremy Tinder**    USA    78-85

Jeremy Tinder is a Chicago-based artist. He primarily makes paintings and comics. Jeremy teaches at The School of the Art Institute of Chicago, Marwen Foundation, and Evanston Art Center. He is a proud member of both the collborative comics collective Trubble Club and the installation/performance group Paintallica.

**Peter Morris**    USA    86-103

Pocketwookie is an artistic force always looking to explore new ideas with an open mind and a sense of humor. He's just as comfortable shaking hands under the bright lights of a gallery opening as he is sharing a drink in a dimly lit gin joint.
He's recognized for his custom repeating patterns, delicious custom toys, unique packaging, children's books and plush toys. His toys, posters, shirt and skateboard designs have been shown in galleries in France, Korea, Canada and Germany, Japan, Israel, Singapore, Germany and England.Pocketwookie is always working hard and sharing the love.

**burunDANGA**    Venezuela    104-129

"Diseñar en nuestra forma de comunicarnos, lo que buscamos es hacerle llegar a las personas de una manera diferente los que llevamos dentro. Crear es nuestra fuente de energía" burunDANGA Design.
Daniel Rinaldi y Alina Izquierdo ya se habían graduado. Los dos ejercían su profesión con éxito. Pero sentían que algo faltaba; hasta que se conocieron y se dieron cuenta que compartían la misma inquietud de diseñar para comunicarse.
Fue así como en el 2006 nace burunDANGA DESIGN una marca innovadora, versátil y fuera de serie que crea productos originales capaces de transmitir el pensamiento versátil, espontáneo e innovador de la dupla.

## Charles Rodriguez   Venezuela   130-135
Lives in Caracas - Venezuela, studied at the School of Visual Arts Cristóbal Rojas. He has worked as an senior art director since 2002 in advertising companies such as Draft FCB, Ogilvy, JMC/Y&R, ARS DDB and Eastwood & Bronson. In 2012 started his intervention as an artist in the Art Toy movement. In 2013 joined the Red Mutuca art collective. Use A.K.A "Gorgocho" on social networks.

## Julia & Guillaume Lachambre   France   136-157
Julia & Guillaume Lachambre AKA Artmymind, two graphic designers and art toy makers based in Paris, France. Their work is collected and has been featured in Art galleries worldwide (New York, San Fransisco, London ,Singapore, etc...). The birth of Artmymind originated in Tokyo,Japan, where the creative duo spent a year studying and feeding their creativity on its mithology and pop art.This translate in their creations being heavily inspired by the Asian culture.

## Doctor A   UK   158-169
Bruce Whistlecraft (A.K.A Doktor A) has become synonymous with the creation of Victorian Futurist style Robot characters.
His popular ongoing Mechtorians series reveals the story of the retrobotic realm of Retropolis one artwork at a time.
Brass mustachioed scientists rub copper-plated elbows with polished metal bank managers, fairground hawkers and socialites in this fantastical realm where humans play no part.
Having exhibited in gallery shows from L.A. to Japan, the Doktor's works have found homes in high profile private art collections around the world and new pieces are keenly anticipated. His characters have also reached a wider audience through the medium of toys.
Doktor A works from his studio on the Yorkshire moors in the UK.

## Blok Design   Canada   170-179
Blok is a multi-disciplinary design studio that specializes in brand identity and brand experiences, editorial design, digital design, packaging, exhibition design and installations. Collaborating with highly creative thinkers from around the world, they take on initiatives that blend cultural awareness, a love of art and humanity to advance society and business alike. Blok's work has received critical recognition around the world and has been exhibited in museums from Tokyo to Toronto.

## Hand in Factory   Korea   180-209
Hands In Factory, the Art Toy team of Coolrain Studio in South Korea.Team is composed of UpTeMPO (Designer) and RocKOON (Modeler).
We are designing characters, producing art toys and other products based on our own design.

## How2work   Hong Kong, China   210-219
How2work was founded in 2001 with the passion and expertise in creation of high quality figures and collectibles. We act as the design catalyst and specialize in transforming images to 3D products. Through the years, How2work collaborated with artists around the world to extend the creative synergy across boundaries. We are dedicated to design work of the highest caliber, with utmost attention to detail and client satisfaction.

## iROC   USA   220-223
 iROC is based out of California USA. His artist back ground is tattooing full time, graffitAnd sculpting.

## Kitra   Romania   224-229
Born in 1981, Kitra lives and works in Bucharest. He is an illustrator, toy designer and street artist. He studied graphics at the University of Arts in Bucharest. Kitra uses various modes of expression, from digital technology to painting, drawing and objects. He prefers not to have a pre-established visual direction so that the "creation process may proceed by itself, naturally"

## Mighty Jaxx   Singapore   230-233
Established in 2012 and based in Singapore
Mighty Jaxx creates highly collectible art figurines using state-of-the-art technology. Founded in 2012 by Jackson Aw, Mighty Jaxx's mission is to turn extraordinary ideas into reality. Collaborating with renowned international artists, we produce outstanding art figures with exceptional quality. Our figures are sculpted digitally and using rapid prototyping we are able to produce a prototype figure in lightning fast time. Working with a professional and ethical factory, our collectibles are produced in China and distributed worldwide through distributors and retailers.

## Monsta   France   234-239
Monsta is a french mixed-media artist living and working in Lyon (France).Through his questionning, he's looking for a way to escape a pretty sad reality, and tries to awaken our chillhood side inside of us as a way-out.
Monsta takes a gloomy and critical look at our society not forgetting to bring a touch of naivety and derision.
A contrasting universe appears under his pencil stroke, the imagination of a (lost) child, where games stand alongside death, where monsters are both cute and terrifying and where dreams blend into nightmares.
He uses different ways to express all these contradictions, whether it be drawing, painting, or sculpture and installation.

### NEVERCREW    Switzerland    240-267
NEVERCREW is a swiss based street artists duo (Christian Rebecchi & Pablo Togni). They work together since 1996 and they mainly work with mural paintings, installations and scultpure.

### The Deisgn Mall    Hong Kong, China    268-277
TDM (The Design Mall) is committed to promote The creation, we cooperate with different Design and creative production of all kinds of interesting and novel products. Attended The multiple large and small exhibitions and activities. In 2011, TDM become more Hong Kong polytechnic university, the first "polyu micro fund plan group (enterprise)" one of the winners.

### Bunka    France    278-289
Yann le Neve, aka Bunka, is a multi-talented artist, toy designer, illustrator, graphic artist... He created a whole world based on the toy characters he produces: the Chaos Monkeys. His work has been inspired by American indie artists such as Mike Mignola or Eric Powell.

### César Zanardi    Argentina    290-295
www.cesarzanardi.com.ar    www.facebook.com/mundo.cerrito

César Zanardi is a Graphic Designer and illustrator born in Buenos Aires, Argentina. He works very actively in Argentina and Japan as Art Director in several areas such as Package Design, Character Design and other artistic projects which include pop pieces such as Art Toys, Merchandising and CD Jackets.
César Zanardi's works are full of symbolic and iconic content, organic atmospheres, animal topics and hints of humor!

### D'creativeaholic    Singapore    296-299
www.dcreativeaholic.com

D'creativeaholic is an indie brand created by Artist Shenly Yee and is derived from the words "The Creative Workaholic". The words carry the mission which is a workaholic with a burning passion for creative design and will never give up his/her dreams no matter what diffculties they face. Her work has been exhibited in various countries - Malaysia/Singapore/Taiwan/Macao/U.K. and were well received.
Most of the artworks are influenced by the beauty of abstract parasitic life forms and the nature that surrounds us. She uses her artwork to bring joy and happiness to herself and hope that it will make others smile too!

### CLOGTWO    Singapore    300-305
THE INK & CLOG

Ink&Clog is the emergence of two individuals, Inkten and Clogtwo, a graphic artist and graffiti writer respectively, whom they have decided to collide in regardless of the atomic law of physics that they have been potentially concealed over 7 years, breaking from the norm. Their body of works involves the exploration of vast medium, touching into digitalcomplexity to the conceptuality of fine arts painting. Seven years of silent construction, this is Ink&Clog.

### Tomasz Płonka    Poland    306-309
Cartoons, comics and animations - it is a fundamental base for my inspirations. I'm filled of even overwhelmed by those images, figures and storylines. Nowadays I seldom read comics or watch cartoons. But it is hard to throw it away from my head. So more self-aware I filled it up with low brow culture, different artist and visions. I noticed that I like cracks, mutations, accumulations and eclosions. And I'm trying to catch the moment of transformation in the very moment.
Just before the end or beginning of something else.
All DIY vinyl toys were made for Vinylcanvas.com

### TAKAO    Japan    310-313
Being inspired by American Comics & Graffiti Art at a young age, he developed his original style that passes through between Comical and Street vibes. Since then, he has produced illustrations, artwork cover & etc for various musicians and he was awakened to Modeling Design a few years ago.Now, he expands the range of activities from illustrations to cubic designs and his work became the talk in Japan & at abroad.He is currently producing collaboration works with his friends' musicians such as HIFANA, DJ KENTARO, KIREEK & etc…

### VISEone    Germany    314-323
Wolfgang Ohlig alias VISEone (born 1969) is an international known urban artist who is well known for his vinyltoy custom works and embraced within the toy niche, as well as crossing over to influential design media like Notcot and Design You Trust.
His works are very successful and have been exhibited in shows worldwide.
Since 2008 VISEone his character design produced some limited edition, and has quickly sold out. By the end of 2013, he got asked by the magazine "CLOSER" Creating vinyltoy Customs to be auctioned at a charity event in Munich.

Ziqi    Singapore    324-327
Chris Alexander    Scotland UK
facebook.com/monsterlittle.ziqi    monsterlittle.com    facebook.com/creodesign

Ziqi (Goh Jit Hee) is the creator of QiQi. He is a Malaysian artist based in Singapore. He specialises in designing cute and fun characters inspired by his love for Japanese style. One of his dreams is to create a character empire which everyone loves.
Chris Alexander is the maker and producer of character driven art and works under the name of Creo Design. Based in Scotland, UK, Chris works independently to produce unique and original art multiples based on his own designs or in collaboration with the world's best creatives. Chris is dedicated to making high quality art pieces by hand but has also enjoyed producing vinyl designer toys with QiQi being his personal favourite.

Chocolate Rain    Hong Kong, China    328-335
Chocolate Rain is inspired by childhood dream and wonderland adventure. Each piece is unique and handcrafted with mix medium and special artistic elements. Prudence is the founder and designer graduated MA in Central St. Martins. She received the 2010 Ten Outstanding Designers Award and honored as one of Hong Kong's Ten Outstanding Young Persons in 2012. Chocolate Rain design has exhibited and distributed internationally. In 2010, BRITISH MUSEUM x Chocolate Rain Collection launched in London. Since 2008, Fatina Dreams Ltd was founded in London and ran global licensing projects. Now Chocolate Rain has flagship stores in Hong Kong and Singapore.

Charuca Vargas    Spain    336-343
I'm an artist based in Barcelona .
I have worked with a lot of companies around the world creating characters for them. Nowadays I consecrate most of my time to creating new graphics and characters for my personal project, my own brand Charuca.

AomeHuskyx3    Hong Kong, China    344-367
HuskyKevin. Brand Director of Husky x3, focusing portrait operating for many years, have been invited to attend a different country and industry forums, sharing of experiences. Kevin repeatedly in an advisory capacity for the development of international brands in the country to launch licensed merchandise. Diversify their creative type, whether 2D, 3D, painting, text, images are, with pure joy and peace.

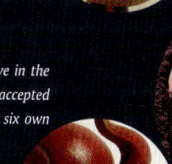

Winson Ma    Hong Kong, China    368-379
Founder of Winson Classic Creation Ltd.Well Known Figure Designer .
In Dec 2005, Winson Ma started his own figure company "Winson Classic Creation". In fact, early in 2000, he was already active in the design industry. He worked with friends to found the figure brand "Brothersfree". He was one of the creative directors. Now, Winson accepted the invitation from Polar Museum Foundation as the art director. He aims to promote the protection of our environmentWCC has six own trademarks, including Apexplorers, Apexworker, Firespecter, Necoco chocolate cat, Polarla and Artdol Family.

13    Taiwan, China    380-391
Born in 1977 in Taiwan ,Illustrator and sculptor .k13toys Design Director.

Bowo Baghaskara    Indonesia    392-401
Bowo Baghaskara is Indonesian Designer Toys. he's also sketch addict, Designer Graphics, Design Character, Painting, Custom Art toys.
End of 2009 he's in as DesignerToys World and created some ArtToys "KUNG POW, BIG BRUNO, DRIAD & UNCLE BRUNO". He's also doing some Custom ArtToys for event project like art & Xhibition,ToysFair or Custom Commission for Collector.
Start from his love of toys and drawing on his childhood, brought him to be one who loves Art.
Concern with condition this nature, became a focus to raise his theme campaign, and spreading the word's : LOVE EARTH" and tried to aplicated into his Artwork.Concern with condition this nature, became a focus to raise his theme campaign, and spreading the word's : LOVE EARTH" and tried to aplicated into his Artwork.

dust    Germany    402-441
dust is a freelance artist and designer with Swiss-German roots. His early work was heavily influenced by the street and urban art scene, adopting the moniker 'dust' in the year 2000. From that point until today, he has been developing his own, unique style.

Aaron Liu    Hong Kong, China    442-445
Blog: http://chaos0115.wordpress.com
He is an architectural and interior designer in Hong Kong. He graduated from architecture program of Carleton University of Ottawa. Founder of creative team "2-Far Playthings". During school he concentrated on building his "paper architecture" into physical forms through found objects, results often demonstrated chaos. He was addicted to the complex and abstract forms ever since. In these processes of destroying and rebuilding unrelated objects, new meanings are given. He uses his hands to think instead of his mind.

## ■■ INSTINCTOY- Gallery Office

INSTINCTOY physical Gallery Office was founded in 2010. The Gallery is a true piece of art, and can display lots of toys. Visitors can feel the sense of design and comfort when entering the Gallery.
In addition to the merchandise, the Gallery has a large collection of dolls and toys from all over the world, making the store also as a must visit place for collectors around the world.

Designer: 大久保博人 (HIROTO OHKUBO)
Country: Japan

## ■■ PASTEKL RAINBOW INC and LIQUID

In 2008, when the first original Inc was launched, it was described as a cute bear and had suffered mysterious liquid monster "LIQUID" erosion. The head was described in spiky looking and has muddy body. This would allow fans to have the freedom to imagine what the Inc could become!

Designer: 大久保博人 (HIROTO OHKUBO)

## ■ Inc

Inc is the year 2008 INSTINCTOY first launch of the original role, after describing a cute bear had suffered mysterious liquid monster "LIQUID" erosion, systemic change dramatically, the head and the body, such as mud burst Cici melt gesture subsequent development would allow fans have inc freedom to imagine it!

Designer: 大久保博人 (HIROTO OHKUBO)

Baby Inc
Designer: 大久保博人
(HIROTO OHKUBO)

## Baby Inc

My son was born when inc continued well received in 2011, at the age he was about to fill a stance very cute, I am standing for the inspiration that redesigned the same dimensions as the baby baby inc, Baby inc first color after the 2013 sale, the second color chocolate baby inc launched in February 2014.

Designer: 大久保博人
(HIROTO OHKUBO)

17

## Baby Inc

Designer: 大久保博人
(HIROTO OHKUBO)

## Mini inc

The sales of the Inc from May 2008 to 2014 proofed the success of the inc and has sold over 2000 units. In response to the popularity of the Inc, the latest mini inc was born thanks to the help of 3D printing technology.

Designer: 大久保博人 (HIROTO OHKUBO)

## LIQUID

LIQUID inc 2008 to commemorate the launch of the sale of minidoll, sold in the form of a strap to show before the erosion inc LIQUID original appearance! To 2014 and now it has launched more than fifty kinds of different colors, for a total sales volume is more than ten thousand of LIQUID popularity can be no better than inc less too!
LIQUID enthusiastic fans is not unusual!

Designer: 大久保博人 (HIROTO OHKUBO)

**LIQUID**
Designer: 大久保博人
(HIROTO OHKUBO)

## LIQUID

Designer: 大久保博人
(HIROTO OHKUBO)

# Muckey
Designer: 大久保博人
(HIROTO OHKUBO)

## Muckey

The 2013 launch of the latest Muckey has the same background story as the Inc. On a day where little bear is sunbathing near the forest suddenly sped up. Muckey's back started to erode and his body color would start to change color by color. What would Muckey's fate be like? Fans would have to use their imagination!

With our latest 3D Modeling technology, the spherical joint structure made of rubber experienced performance expression change. From a second, it was still a cute little bear, and it suddenly turned into a Muckey monster! This is a highly playable and a must get toy!

Designer: 大久保博人 (HIROTO OHKUBO)

# Muckey

Designer: 大久保博人
(HIROTO OHKUBO)

## Muckey

Designer: 大久保博人
(HIROTO OHKUBO)

## ▰▰ Vincent

This is a work for my friend who loves monsters. The character's name itself is taken from my friend, Vincent. Vincent is a mysterious liquid vivo biological LIQUID showdown. It is a large monster with different parts such as the jaw joints, which demonstrate changes in the expression of powerful expression of lost to erosion debilitating the body to adjust the body posture. This can make the big monster stand and lean forward, as the character is about to come alive!

Designer: 大久保博人 (HIROTO OHKUBO)

Vincent

Designer: 大久保博人 (HIROTO OHKUBO)

Vincent
Designer: 大久保博人 (HIROTO OHKUBO)

■■ Vincent

Designer: 大久保博人
(HIROTO OHKUBO)

Designer: 大久保博人 (HIROTO OHKUBO)

Designer: 大久保博人
(HIROTO OHKUBO)

### Lonney

Designer: Roar with Lukas
Country: Austria
Photographer: Axel Gülcher

## Kisho the Urban Medic Ninja

Designer: Roar with Lukas
Country: Austria
Photographer: Axel Gülcher

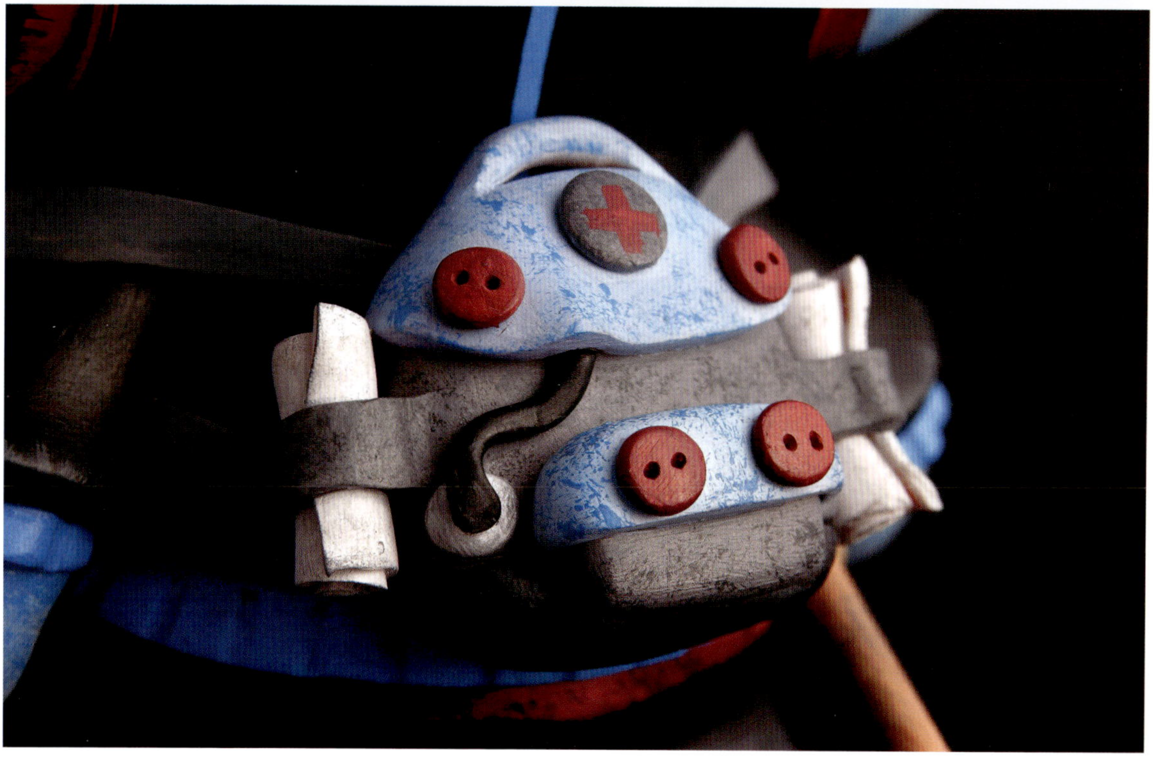

## Dunnys for the Fresh Batch Series

Designer: Roar with Lukas
Country: Austria
Photographer: Axel Gülcher

■■ Dunnys for the Fresh Batch Series

Designer: Roar with Lukas
Country: Austria
Photographer: Axel Gülcher

## Wippo Senior

Designer: Roar with Lukas
Country: Austria
Photographer: Axel Gülcher

## Taimu

Designer: Roar with Lukas
Country: Austria
Photographer: Axel Gülcher

59

## Many characters

Designer: Yow
Country: JAPAN

# ■■■ INVADERS

Designer: Yow
Country: JAPAN
Material: Resin casting, Polymer clay, vinyl
INVADERS (25cm)

## ■■ SCREAM HUMAN SKULL

Designer: Yow
Country: JAPAN
Material: Resin casting, Polymer clay, vinyl
INVADERS (25cm)

65

Title: Booby Faces
Designer: Yow

Title: Lucky Devil
Designer: Yow

Title: Sarry
Designer: Yow

Title: Mars maddy
Designer: Yow

**Too weird to ride SK8 deck**

Designer: Yow
Country: JAPAN
Material: Wood,Resin casting,Polymer clay
CUSTOM SKATE BORD

Title: Ahh

### CAP DUCK-FRANKENSTEIN GID

Special design for Halloween.
SIZE : approximate16.5CM

Designer: SHON
Country: Taiwan, China
Photographer: SHON

## Cap Devil

Cap devil is a new character appear during Cap duck's running journey.
The soul of other dead ducks gather together becoming Cap Devil, to obstruct cap duck running.
170mm tall / edition size 10

Title: CAP DUCK BLACK/GRAY

Title: CAP DUCK-PINK GID Hong Kong Limited

Title: CAP DUCK PINK

## CAP DUCK RABBIT

Follow the storyline about cap duck, he keep running from BOSS's catching until winter.
Cap duck camouflage a rabbit, but it's too cold and snow white out, he was frozen and become white all over the body….
170mm tall / edition size 12

Designer: SHON

## Cup Duck the 4th Anniversary Edition

Cup Duck the 4th Anniversary Edition
Electropulated in gold color.
170mm tall / edition size 6
Celebrating Cap duck was 4-years old.

## WAR BABY PAINTING GID

War baby is a character who begun life in a comic strip that SHON cooperate with a Taiwan fashion brand "UNDER PEACE".
Baby is a symbol of pure and innocent.
Otherwise a baby wearing a gas mask just to show he wants to prevent an outside pollution and SHON make it to declare his Anti-War position.
170mm tall / edition size 13

## Cap Duck ElK

At christmas day, SHON made this Cap duck elk to celebrate.
He also put this work in a crystal ball (not real crystal just looks like it ) increasing an atmosphere of Christmas.
SIZE : 8.5CM

Design Agency: www.mydearbilly.com
Creative Director: Billy Mac Donald
Design Director: Billy Mac Donald
Country: Ireland
Designer: Billy Mac Donald
Photographer: Billy Mac Donald

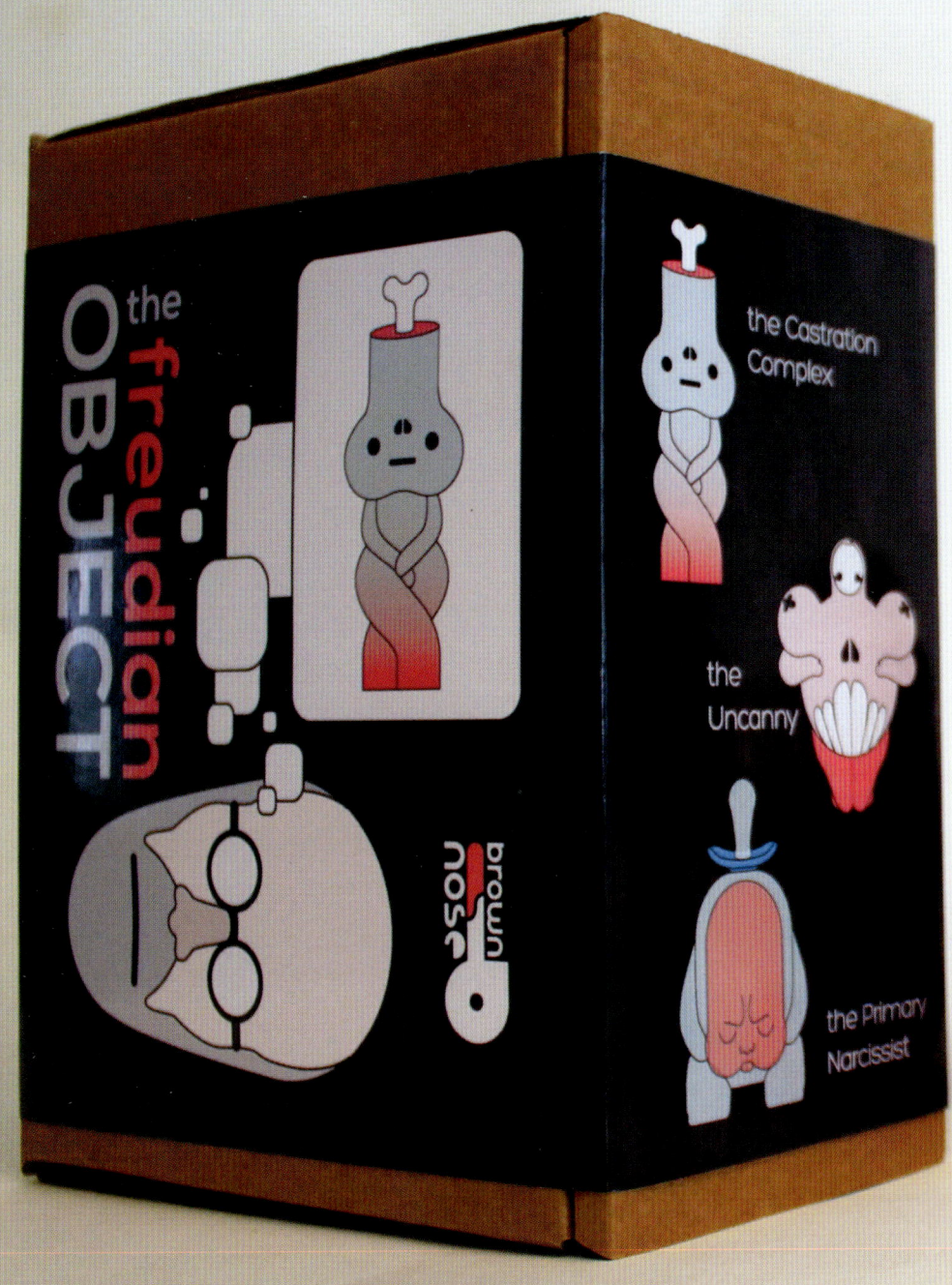

## The Freudian OBJECT

The Freudian OBJECT is a set of three designer toys. They each embody one of Sigmund Freud's psychoanalytic concepts. The Freudian OBJECTs are artifacts of the unconscious taking the form of The Uncanny, The Castration Complex and The Primary Narcissist.

"The psychoanalyst, like the archaeologist, must uncover layer after layer of the patient's psyche, before coming to the deepest, most valuable treasures."
~ Sigmund Freud

They stand approx 7" tall, cast in solid polyurethane resin and are packaged in a diecut cardboard box with a glossy sleeve which doubles as a poster.

Each toy includes an edition card with a unique edition number & signature.

## The Freudian OBJECT

Designer: Billy Mac Donald

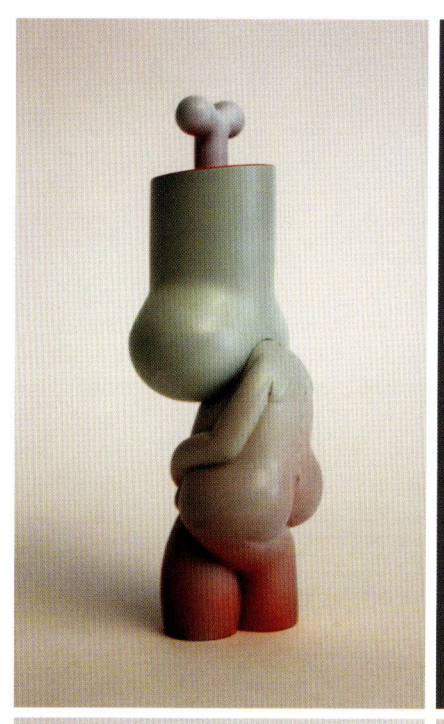
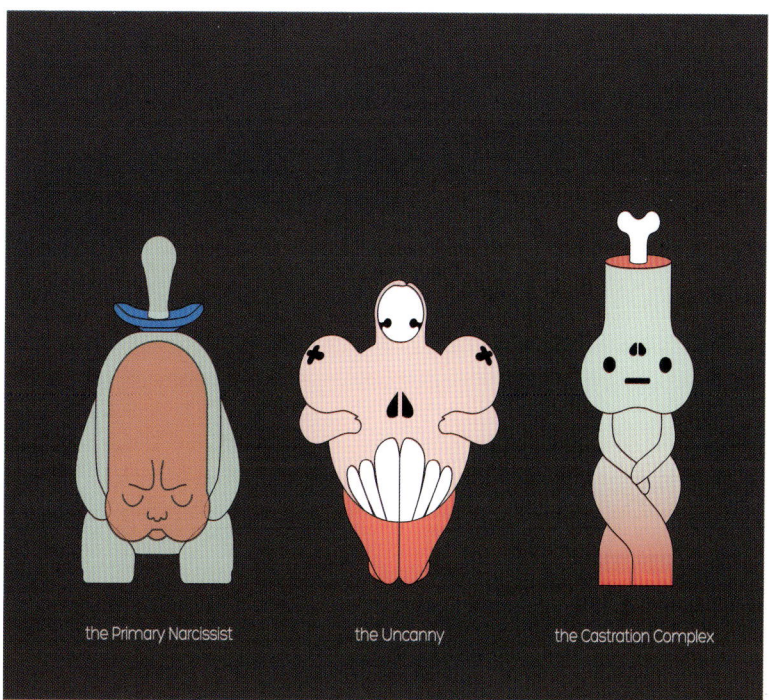

the Primary Narcissist     the Uncanny     the Castration Complex

## Tinder Toys

The Tinder Toys are three designer toy mini-figures based on the artwork of Chicago-based artist Jeremy Tinder and produced by Squibbles Ink + Rotofugi.

Design Agency: Squibbles Ink + Rotofugi
Creative Director: Jeremy Tinder
Design Director: Kirby Kerr
Designer: Jeremy Tinder
Country: USA

## Tinder Toys

Boyger is a very happy young man. He has mastered the art of burger making and simply wants to share his creations with the world. Every morning, Boyger rises, pours himself a cup of coffee and heads out to his grill. Once a perfectly formed burger is placed atop his head, Boyger is ready to face the day. If you see him please compliment his burger, it will make his day.

## Tinder Toys

Clem was born out of an unlikely circumstance. Initially thought to be merely the world's largest orange, Clem had a secret hidden within. As Florida state fair judges closely examined the overgrown citrus, they heard cries of despair reverberating inside the orange! Upon cutting it open, a face was revealed and a body unfurled! Clem is the first known of his kind, a citrus-sapien. His tears and sweat are delicious.

## ■■ Tinder Toys

Rabburt is not a typical bunny. Deep down, he's a good guy, but he is easily put on edge. It's not his fault, it's yours. Quit asking him stupid questions, don't bother him when he's watching his shows and stop chewing with your mouth open. Follow his rules and you'll be Rabburt's best friend.

# Pocketwookie

Design Agency: pocketwookie
Designer: Peter Morris
Client: KidRobot, Toy2R
Photographer: Peter Morris
Country: USA

## Pocketwookie

Designer: Peter Morris

## Pocketwookie

Designer: Peter Morris

## Pocketwookie

Designer: Peter Morris

### Pocketwookie

Designer: Peter Morris

# Pocketwookie

Designer: Peter Morris

## Pocketwookie

Designer: Peter Morris

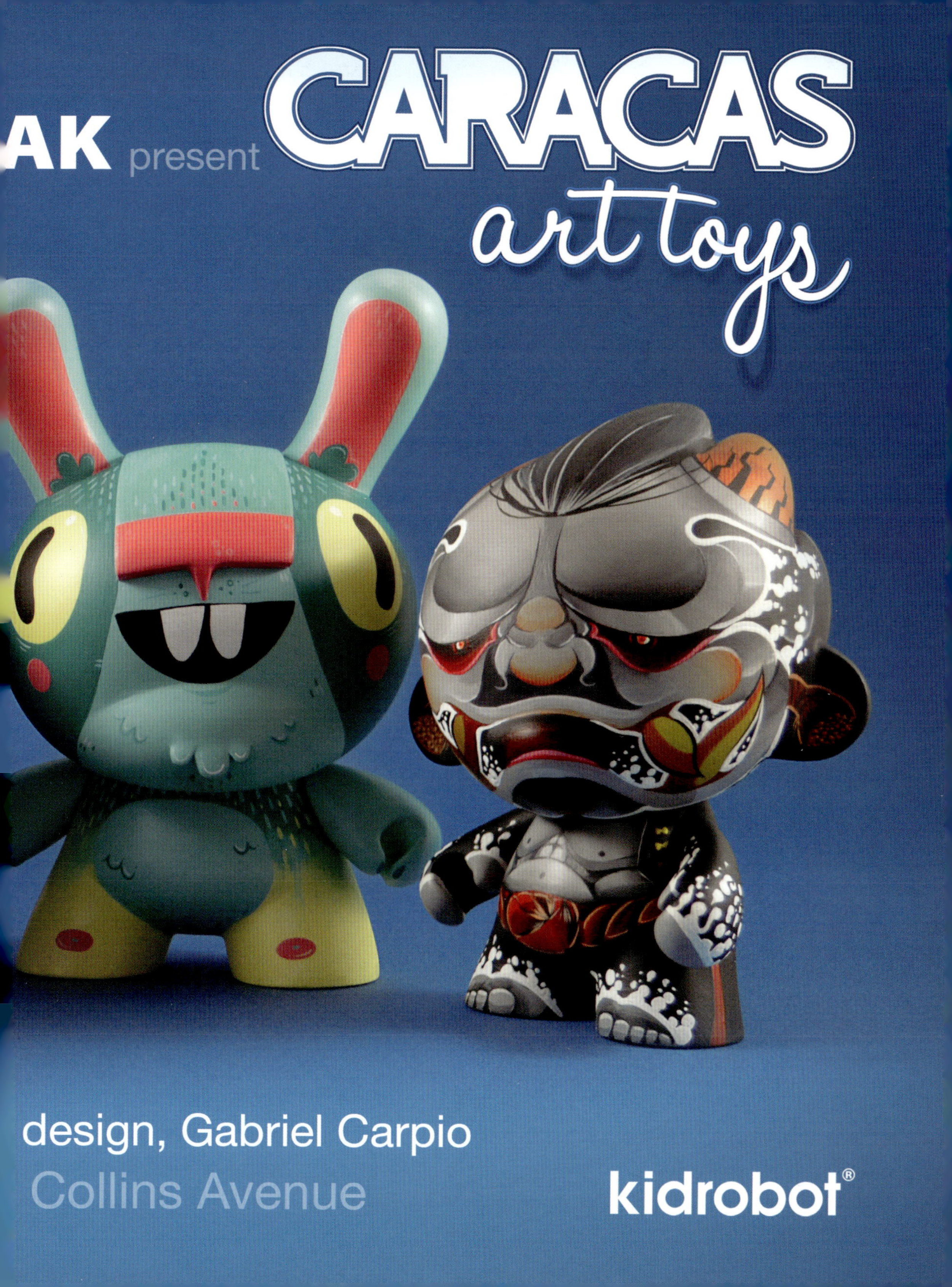

**AK** present **CARACAS** *art toys*

design, Gabriel Carpio
Collins Avenue

**kidrobot**®

## DUNNY

This piece are created for the Show "CARACAS Art Toys" at Kidrobot Miami.

Design Agency: burunDanga
Greative Director: burunDanga
Design Director: burunDanga
Country: Venezuela
Designer: Aly Izquierdo
Client: personal
Photographer: burunDanga design
Platform: DUNNY 7"
Materials: Acrylic paint and Magic Sculpt on vinyl

Rabbit gazpacho is an exotic food, we do not eat rabbit but we think it would be fun putting this name.
For this Show we add a new color to our palette, the SEAWATER!!! And is now our new favorite.

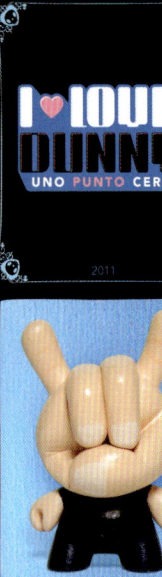

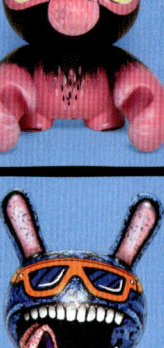
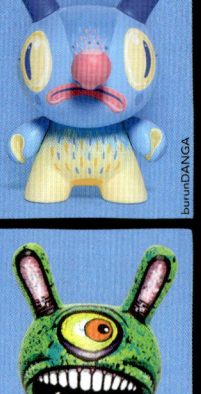

Designer: Aly Izquierdo

Designer: Aly Izquierdo

Designer: Aly Izquierdo

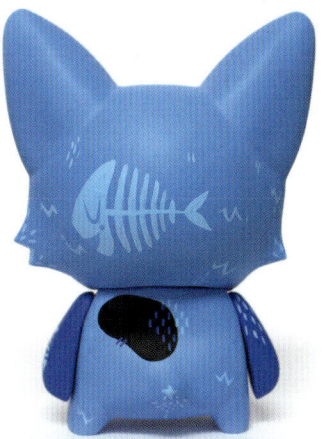

## ▬▬ ▬ ▪ BENITO

Benito is inspired by a real life cat, It is the first cat of my best friend. We love to use blue color, and combined with black and pink is one of our favorite mixes. And we had the pleasure of designing the poster of the event. This piece are created for the Show "FONZO LOVE NY" at my Plastic Heart.

Design Agency: burunDanga
Creative Director: burunDanga
Design Director: burunDanga
Country: Venezuela
Designer: Aly Izquierdo
Client: personal
Photographer: burunDanga design
Platform: FONZO 6"
Materials: Acrylic paint and Magic Sculpt on vinyl

## MISHU

Mishu is an Italian stray cat with an athletic physique jajajajaja
This piece are created for the Show "Fonzo loves California" at Dragatomi , Sacramento CA.

Platform: FONZO 6"
Materials: Acrylic paint and Magic Sculpt on vinyl

## TOPOLLILLO
### Intergalactic

The topollillo is a mad creature, does not belong to this world, has two radical personalities.
This piece are created for the Show "I LOVE FONZO" at Freak Store - Venezuela.

Platform: FONZO 6"
Materials: Acrylic paint and Magic Sculpt on vinyl

## The Blue PUG

This pug was inspired by the pug of a friend, their Big and funny eyes, its small ears.
This piece are created for the Show "Fonzo loves The UK" at The SHO gallery.

Platform: FONZO 6"
Materials: Acrylic paint and Magic Sculpt on vinyl

# MEOW cat

This piece are created for the Show "CARACAS Art Toys" at Kidrobot Miami.

Platform: Munny 7"
Materials: Acrylic paint and Magic Sculpt on vinyl and FONZO diy ears.

## Labbit

This piece are created for the Show "CARACAS Art Toys" at Kidrobot Miami.

Design Agency: burunDanga
Creative Director: burunDanga
Design Director: burunDanga
Country: Venezuela
Designer: Aly Izquierdo
Client: personal
Photographer: burunDanga design
Name: Rabbit and Poop
Platform: Labbit 10"
Materials: Acrylic paint and Magic Sculpt on vinyl

■■■ MANDY the old devil

Mandy is the old devil .
This piece are created for the Show "I LOVE MUNNY 2.0" at my Freak Store. Caracas - Venezuela.

Design Agency: burunDanga
Greative Director: burunDanga
Design Director: burunDanga
Country: Venezuela
Designer: Aly Izquierdo
Client: personal
Photographer: burunDanga design
Platform: Mini Raffy and mini Trikky
Materials: Acrylic paint and Magic Sculpt on vinyl

## The monster of Mucubají Lake

Mucubají lagoon, is a mysterious lake which is located in Merida Venezuela. This monster lives there, in a very cold place. We again use the aquamarine as a basis for our inspiration. This piece are created for the Show "CARACAS Art Toys" at Kidrobot Miami.

Design Agency: burunDanga
Greative Director: burunDanga
Design Director: burunDanga
Country: Venezuela
Designer: Aly Izquierdo
Client: personal
Photographer: burunDanga design
Platform: Kid Neutron 8" + Munny 7"
Materials: Acrylic paint and Magic Sculpt on vinyl

## UGA UGA

This munny is a Pink monkey created for the Show Caracas Art Toys at Kidrobot Miami, love PINK!

Design Agency: burunDanga
Greative Director: burunDanga
Design Director: burunDanga
Country: Venezuela
Designer: Aly Izquierdo
Client: personal
Photographer: burunDanga design
Platform: Munny 7"
Materials: Acrylic paint and Magic Sculpt on vinyl

Title: Kakortok   Designer: Charles Rodriguez

Title: Amarok   Designer: Charles Rodriguez

Title: Rock Hand   Designer: Charles Rodriguez

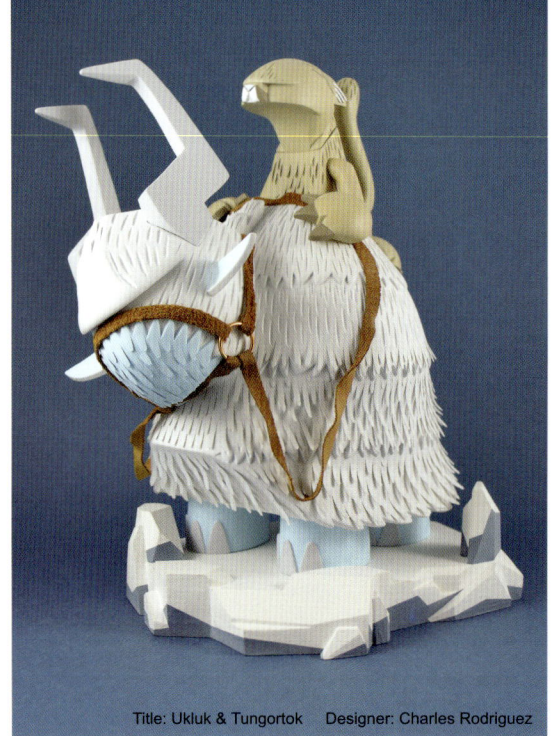

Title: Ukluk & Tungortok   Designer: Charles Rodriguez

# Afro Sheep

Designer: Charles Rodriguez

Title: Tupit   Designer: Charles Rodriguez

Title: Gari   Designer: Charles Rodriguez

Title: Takeo   Designer: Charles Rodriguez

Title: Nanook   Designer: Charles Rodriguez

# Abidu

Designer: Charles Rodriguez

## Maximus

Designer: Charles Rodriguez

## Shikko Sha

Limited edition custom 3 "Dunny series"
Acrylics, resin, Synthetic hair & Fabrics on vin.

Design Agency: Artmymind
Creative Director: Guillaume Lachambre
Design Director: Guillaume Lachambre
Country: France
Designer: Julia&Guillaume Lachambre
Photographer: Guillaume Lachambre

# 3 Samurais

Created for a private collector, these 3 pieces were handcrafted, hand-tailored and hand-painted on 7"Blank viny Dunny, Munny and Trikky figures from Kidrobot.
Epoxy clay, Acrylics, Fabrics, wood on vinyl.

Design Agency: Artmymind
Creative Director: Guillaume Lachambre
Design Director: Guillaume Lachambre
Country: France
Designer: Julia&Guillaume Lachambre
Photographer: Guillaume Lachambre

## Japanese Cake toppers

Privately commissioned wedding cake toppers.
Acrylics, fabrics & resin on vinyl.

Designer: Julia&Guillaume Lachambre

## Hinobatsu

Handcrafted 8 Dunny for the Most Wanted:Behind the show at 1AM San Francisco.
Polymer , Acrylics , Fabrics on vinyl.

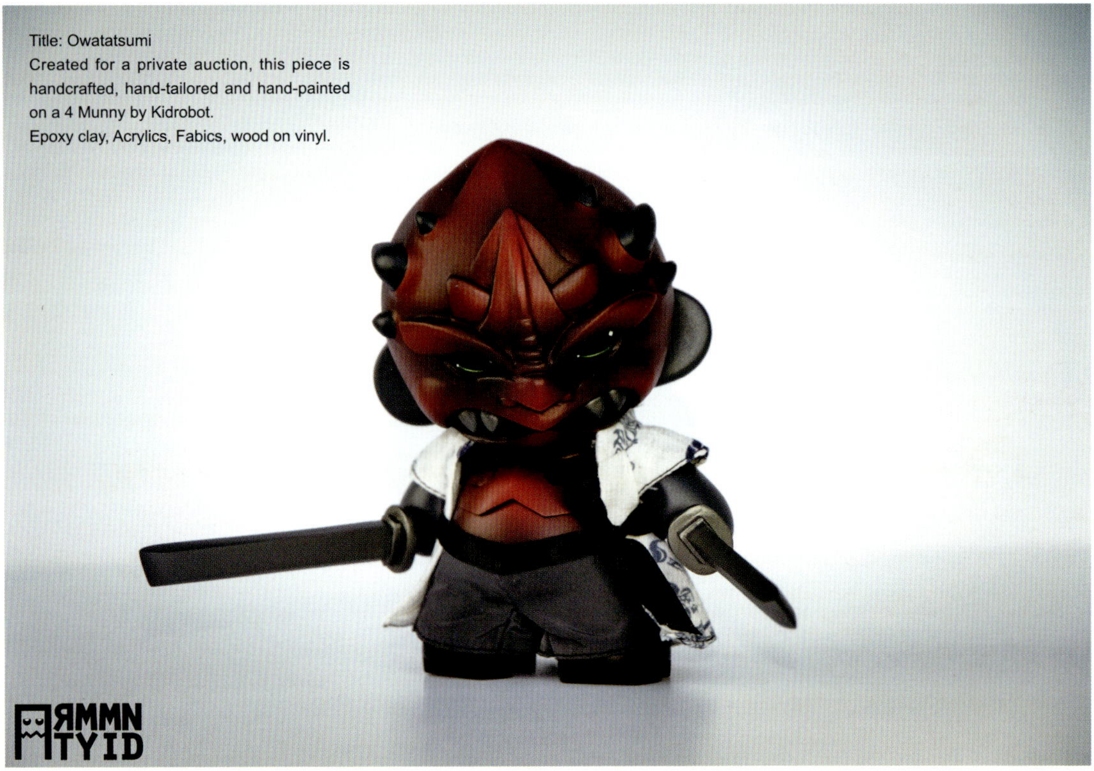

Title: Owatatsumi
Created for a private auction, this piece is handcrafted, hand-tailored and hand-painted on a 4 Munny by Kidrobot.
Epoxy clay, Acrylics, Fabics, wood on vinyl.

Title: Gate Keeper
Created a limited edition custom 4 Munny series. The day darkness will rise once again stronger than ever, our world will endure it's most desperate times. But on the edge of extinction, an opposite force will appear and in apocalyptic battle, face the thousand fangs.
Epoxy, Acrylics; Fabrics, Synthetic Acrylics & Resin on vinyl.

Title: Katsu
Privately commissioned Custom 8 Dunny.
Polymer, Acrylics, Resin & Fabrics on vinyl

Title: Kuroi Ookami

Title: Higitsune

Title: Moliko
Custom 4 Kidrobot Munny.
Acrylics, Fabrics, Resin, Synthetic Hair and wood on vinyl

# Chusa Ankoku

Handcrafted, hand-tailored and hand-painted Custom 4 Munny.
Chusa Ankoku... A name feared on the battleground by his enemy as much as his own men. His blade slash through everything crossing his path, driven by an inextinguishable rage. Only one thing matters..Who stays up at the end of the day and who rots on the ground.
Epoxy, Acrylics, 7 resin.

Designer: Julia&Guillaume Lachambre

Title: Chusa Ankoku

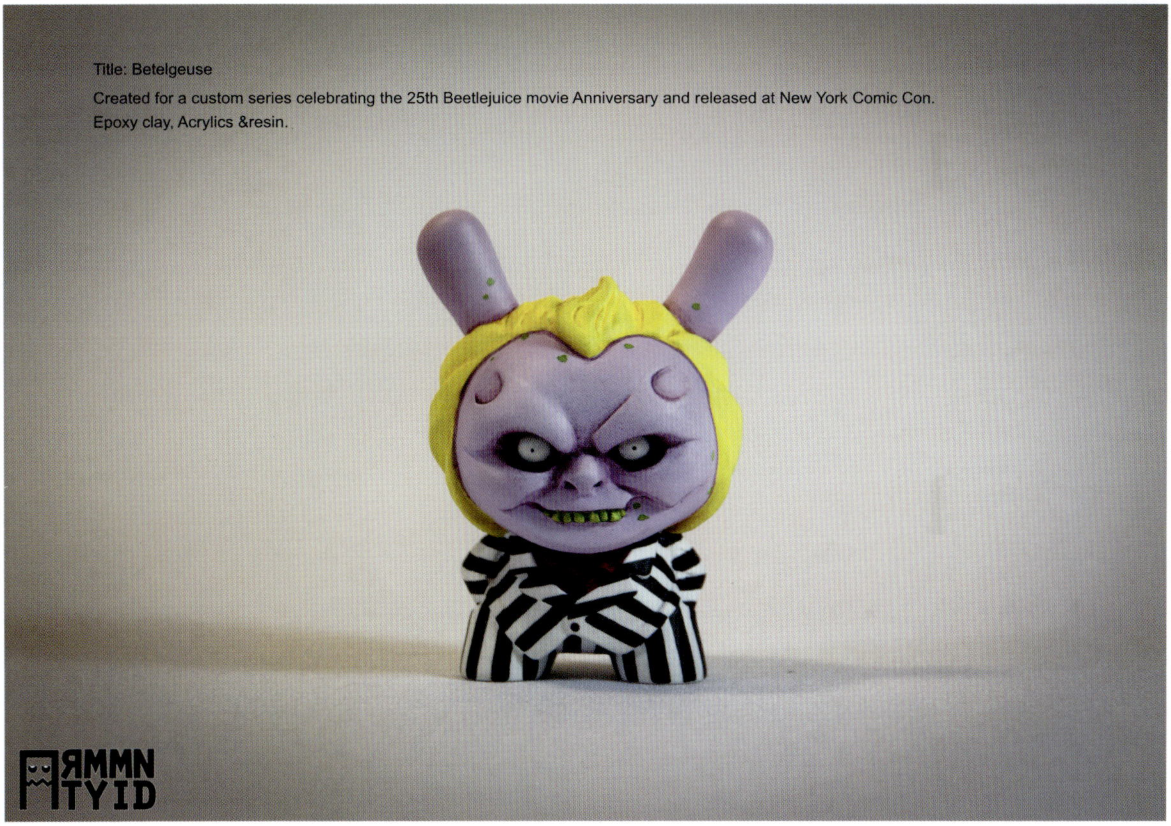

Title: Betelgeuse
Created for a custom series celebrating the 25th Beetlejuice movie Anniversary and released at New York Comic Con.
Epoxy clay, Acrylics &resin.

## ■ ■ Ashbringer

"Ashbringer" privately commissioned custom Muttpop Tequila
"The night is cold and shadows rule over the realm. He stands, looking at waht is left from the brutal battle that ripped this land apart. The incendiary rage as left his molten heart and of his foes, only ashes remain. Cruel like no other Infernal flames claimed the life of thousands, melting steel and consuming souls."
Epoxy clay, Acrylics on vinyl.

Created as a limited edition custom 3"Dunny series.
"In life, we served. In death, we serve. The night is ours and your nightmares, our blood"
Epoxy, Acrylics, & resin.

Title: Chimamire

Title: Drakan Blackfire & Krann Fangbreaker

### Owatatsumi

Handcrafted 8 Dunny for the Most Wanted&Behind the show at 1AM San Francisco.
Polymer, Acrylics, Fabics on vinyl.

Designer: Julia&Guillaume Lachambre

Title: Romeo

Title: Evil Business

Title: Hellhound

Title: Tengu

Title: Storm Samurai

## Ulrich Von Boomboom

Custom 6 Dynamite Rex Raaar for the "Raaar" show at Clutter Gallery in New York.
Epoxy, Acrilics & Wood on Vinyl.
Designer: Julia&Guillaume Lachambre

## Laughing Dead_ Breaking Mad

Privately commissioned Custom 8 Kidrobot Dunny.
Epoxy & Acrylics on vinyl.

## Isamu Tora

Handcrafted custom10 Muttpop King Katch.
Polymer, Aylics, Fabrics on vinyl.

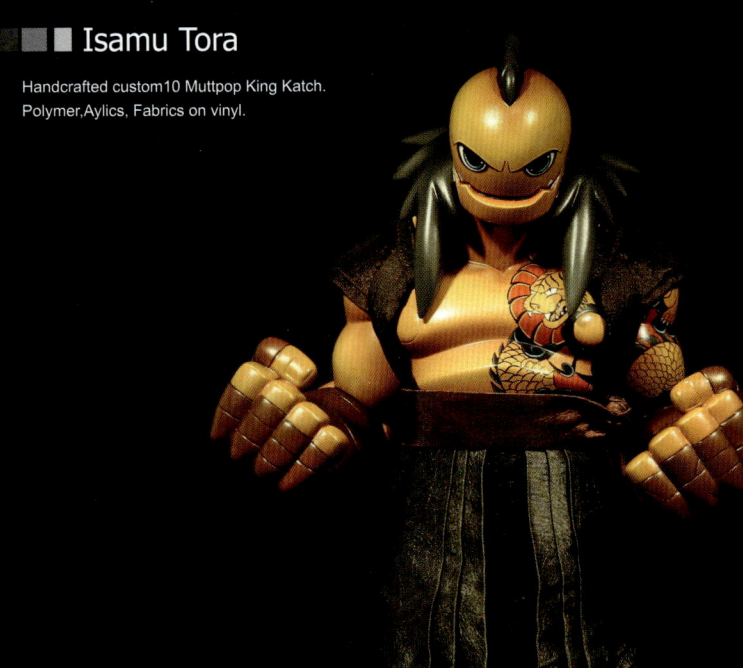

## Storm Samurai

Privately commissioned custom 4 Kidrobot Munny.

Inspired by the Iconic Star Wars Stormtrooper mashed-up with a stylised Samurai armor. The collision of two cultures, past and contemporary merged in one design.

Designer: Julia&Guillaume Lachambre

## Mechtorian toys

Country: UK
Designer: Doktor A. ( Bruce Whistlecraft )
Photographer: Doktor A.

## ■■ Mechtorian toys

Designer: Doktor A. ( Bruce Whistlecraft )

## Mechtorian toys

Designer: Doktor A. ( Bruce Whistlecraft )

## Mechtorian toys

Designer: Doktor A. ( Bruce Whistlecraft )

## Mechtorian toys
Designer: Doktor A. ( Bruce Whistlecraft )

## Mechtorian toys

Designer: Doktor A. ( Bruce Whistlecraft )

Design Agency: Blok Design
Creative Director: Vanessa Eckstein, Marta Cutler, Sara Nickleson
Country: Canada
Designer: Kevin Boothe, Emily Tu, Vanessa Eckstein
Photographer: Arash Moallemi

## This is not a toy

"This Is Not A Toy" an exhibit at the Design Exchange Museum, explores the boundaries between contemporary art, culture and toys. Guest curated by Pharrell Williams, the show features works by Takashi Muyrakami and Koz. The identity and the exhibit graphics needed to honour the subject while providing a sophisticated counterpoint that left space for the individual pieces to shine.

Designer: Kevin Boothe, Emily Tu, Vanessa Eckstein

## RUNNING HORNS

Agency : HANDS IN FACTORY
Creative Director : RocKOON (Taejun Park)
Design Director : UpTeMPO (Jaeheun Lee)
Designer : UpTeMPO (Jaeheun Lee)
Country : KOREA
Photographer : UpTeMPO & RocKOON

## RUNNING HORNS

Designer : UpTeMPO (Jaeheun Lee)

## ■■ RUNNING HORNS

Designer : UpTeMPO (Jaeheun Lee)

## RUNNING HORNS

Designer : UpTeMPO (Jaeheun Lee)

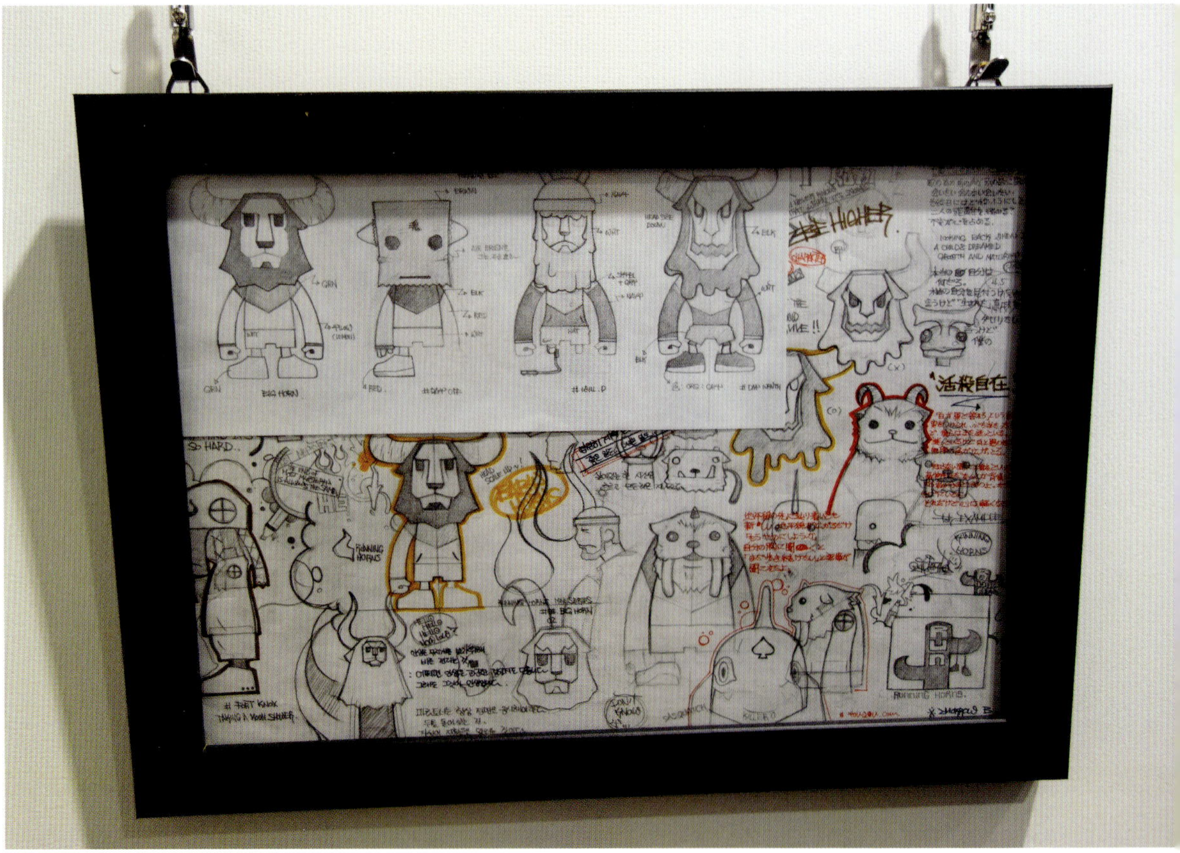

188

# RUNNING HORNS

Designer : UpTeMPO (Jaeheun Lee)

# RUNNING HORNS

Designer : UpTeMPO (Jaeheun Lee)
Custom by Bear King (team FIGURE IN)

Custom by Max Cho

197

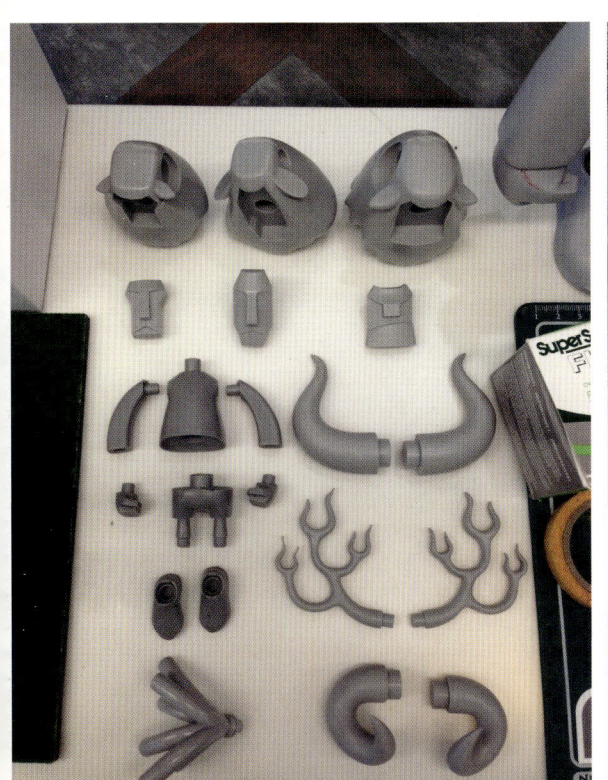

## RUNNING HORNS

Designer : UpTeMPO (Jaeheun Lee)

co-work with FIGURE IN

# RUNNING HORNS

Designer : UpTeMPO (Jaeheun Lee)

204

# ■ RUNNING HORNS

Designer : UpTeMPO (Jaeheun Lee)

# ▮▮▮ RUNNING HORNS

Designer : UpTeMPO (Jaeheun Lee)

# ■■ RUNNING HORNS

Designer : UpTeMPO (Jaeheun Lee)
Custom by Vital9 (Team DUCOBI)
Not Commercial Value. Only respect Stussy.

Custom by Muung (Team DUCOBI)
Not Commercial Value. Only respect Mishika.

# Garden(palm)er 7 Inches Action Figure

Gardner(palm)er 7 Inches figure.
Set of 9 characters + one hidden characte.

Design Agency:  How2work Limited
Creative Director:  Howard Lee
Artist: Michael Lau
Country: Hong Kong, China
Photographer: How2work

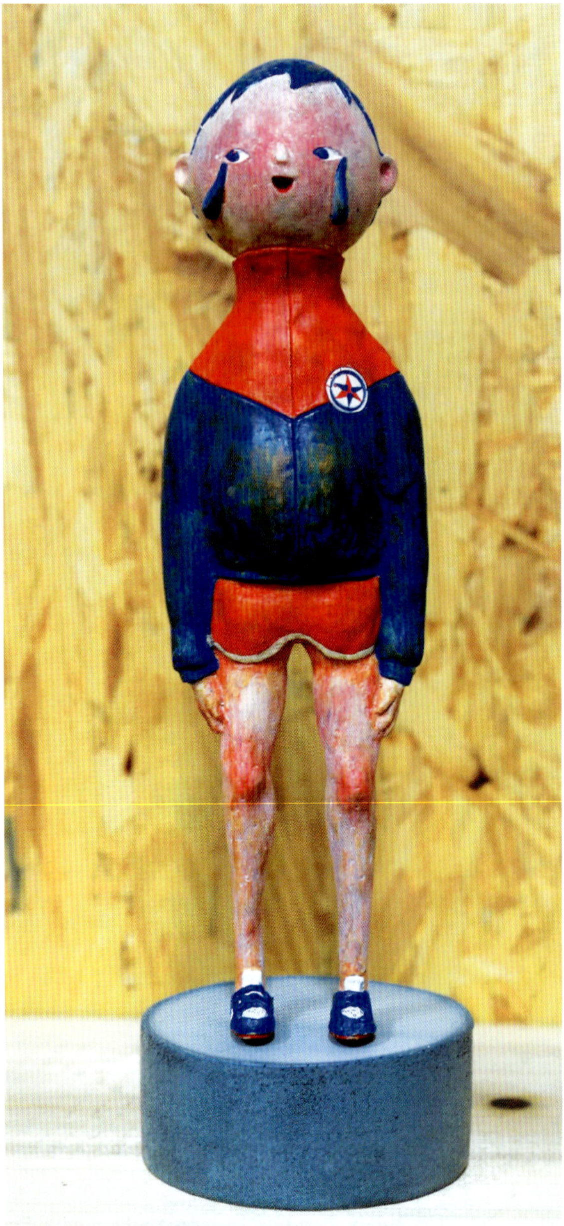

■■ Siu Ming Polystone Figurine    Albert Einstein 1/6 Action Figure

Siu Ming Polystone Figurine

Artist: Kila Cheung

## Le Petit Prince 1/6 Action Figure

Artist: Antoine de Saint-Exupéry

## Mori girl Sculpture

Mori girl Sculpture of Polystone, wood and mixed media with wooden certificate of authenticity
Edition 200 sets

Design Agency: How2work Limited
Creative Director: Howard Lee
Designer: Yoshitomo Nara
Country: Hong Kong, China
Photographer: How2work

### Little My 6 Inches Action Figure

Little My 6 inches figure

**Design Agency:** How2work Limited
**Creative Director:** Howard Lee
**Designer:** Tove Jansson
**Country:** Hong Kong, China
**Photographer:** How2work

## iROC

Designer: Troy Martin "iROC"
Country: USA
Photographer: Troy Martin

## iROC

Designer: Troy Martin "iROC"
Country: USA
Photographer: Troy Martin

## Monsters of Joy

Six toys that I've done is a contrast between joy and the concept of ugliness.

Designer: Kitra & Titi Ciocan
Country: Romania
Photographer: Catalin Grigore

## Skull Bomb

We worked with well known sculptor Jason Freeny (USA) to produce one of his original sculpture, the SKULL BOMB. This is the 4th colour way to be released. Decked in gloss pink with a baby blue stripe and standing at 7.5" tall, the SKULL BOMB is produced using the highest quality polystone, hand painted and packaged into a custom blister and full colour laminated box.

Design Agency: Mighty Jaxx
Creative Director: Jackson Aw
Design Director: Jackson Aw
Designer: Jason Freeny
Country: Singapore

## Mr Hell Yeah

For the very first time, MAMAFAKA's Mr HELLYEAH character as an art collectible! We had teamed up with him to develop this collectible before his unfortunate demise in 2013. This year, with the talented MMFK team and family, we have completed this project, fulfilling MMFK's vision. We are honoured to be part of his legacy. Partial proceeds from the sales will be contributed to his family.

Design Agency: Mighty Jaxx
Creative Director: Jackson Aw
Design Director: Jackson Aw
Designer: MAMAFAKA
Country: Singapore

## Bad Apple

Mighty Jaxx collaborate with prominent French artist GOIN to produce his iconic artwork, Bad Apple into a 3D sculpture. Bad Apple have since sold out worldwide.

Designer: GOIN
Country: Singapore

## <Squad> serie

Handmade toys serie, with different animal's skulls on " kidrobot Munny " vinyl toy base.
(skull, vinyl, acrylic, wood and felt)

Designer: Monsta
Country: France
Photographer: (Monsta)

Designer: Monsta

## <Squad >serie

Designer: Monsta

## ■■■ Dress Code - The Bunny Party

Realized during the contest "Custom" in Vevey, 2010.

Designer: NEVERCREW (Christian Rebecchi & Pablo Togni)
Based on Toy2R "Bunee" Qee
Country: Switzerland
Photographer: NEVERCREW

## Good Morning Beard

The "Good Morning Beard Dunny" is a very limited series hand-made custom included in the "Most Wanted 3" series.

Designer: NEVERCREW (Christian Rebecchi & Pablo Togni)
Based on Kidrobot "Dunny"
Country: Switzerland
Photographer: NEVERCREW

## ■■■ 7 Munny Custom Series

At the end of april 2011 NEVERCREW completed these seven Munny customs (4 inches) for the Munnyworld Megacontest organized by Kidrobot. Their designs were: "Sand snake's dinner" (an "unlucky Munny"), "Living City", "Apartment Bat", "Vampirized" (another "unlucky Munny"), "Munny's Freedom" (the marionette Munny) "Cupboard dweller" and "Concrete cleaner".
The 31th of may 2011, Kidrobot and its judjes announced the list of the winners in each category. The "Vampirized" Munny won in the "Best Minimalist Design" category. In addition, also other two of these customs reached a bit of glory: 2nd place in the "Best Animal Design" category for "Apartment Bat" and 3rd place in the "Most Innovative" category for the "Living City" Munny.

Designer: NEVERCREW (Christian Rebecchi & Pablo Togni)
Based on Kidrobot *Dunny*
Country: Switzerland
Photographer: NEVERCREW

## 7 Munny Custom Series

At the end of april 2011 NEVERCREW completed these seven Munny customs (4 inches) for the Munnyworld Megacontest organized by Kidrobot. Their designs were: "Sand snake's dinner" (an "unlucky Munny"), "Living City", "Apartment Bat", "Vampirized" (another "unlucky Munny"), "Munny's Freedom" (the marionette Munny) "Cupboard dweller" and "Concrete cleaner".
The 31th of may 2011, Kidrobot and its judges announced the list of the winners in each category. The "Vampirized" Munny won in the "Best Minimalist Design" category. In addition, also other two of these customs reached a bit of glory: 2nd place in the "Best Animal Design" category for "Apartment Bat" and 3rd place in the "Most Innovative" category for the "Living City" Munny.

Designer: NEVERCREW (Christian Rebecchi & Pablo Togni)
Based on Kidrobot "Dunny"
Country: Switzerland
Photographer: NEVERCREW

## 7 Munny Custom Series

Designer: NEVERCREW (Christian Rebecchi & Pablo Togni)
Based on Kidrobot "Dunny"
Country: Switzerland
Photographer: NEVERCREW

## The Big Cupboard Dweller

Designer: NEVERCREW (Christian Rebecchi & Pablo Togni)
Based on Kidrobot "Munny"
Country: Switzerland
Photographer: NEVERCREW

# Hangselm

Designer: NEVERCREW (Christian Rebecchi & Pablo Togni)
Country: Switzerland
Photographer: NEVERCREW

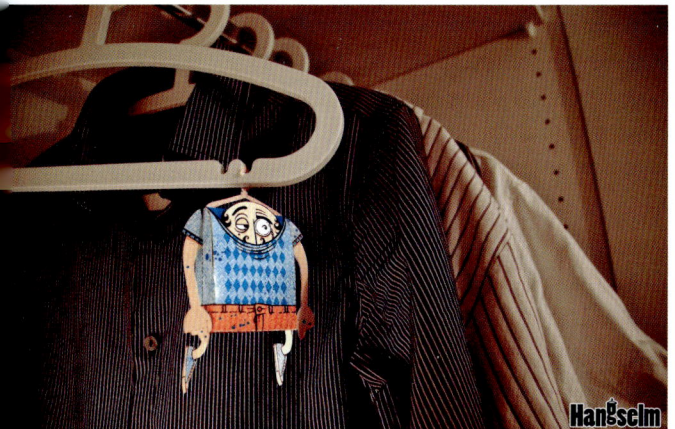

266

267

Pirenche Figure

Title: Little Brownie

## PO! x The Design Mall Friends

TDM (The Design Mall) is committed to promote The creation, we cooperate with different Design and creative production of all kinds of interesting and novel products. Attended The multiple large and small exhibitions and activities. In 2011, TDM become more Hong Kong polytechnic university, the first "polyu micro fund plan group (enterprise)" one of the winners.

Country: Hong Kong, China

# PO! x The Design Mall Friends

PO! x The Design Mall Friends 3" Vinyl figure Series 1

Title: Priotica(special edition)

Title: Smiley Crocodile
(from Taiwan)

Title: Smeraldo

Title: HappiPanda
(from Hong Kong)

Title: 3.14 (from Hong Kong)

Title: Lemi (from Indonesia)

Title: Willowisp

Title: HarshHell GreatHell

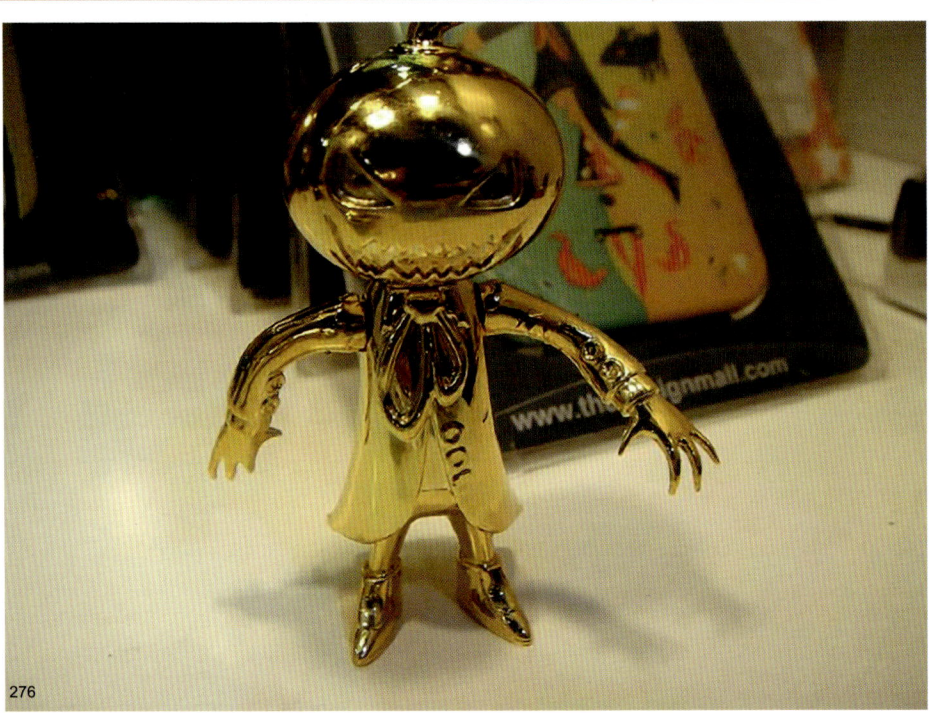

## PO! x The Design Mall Friends

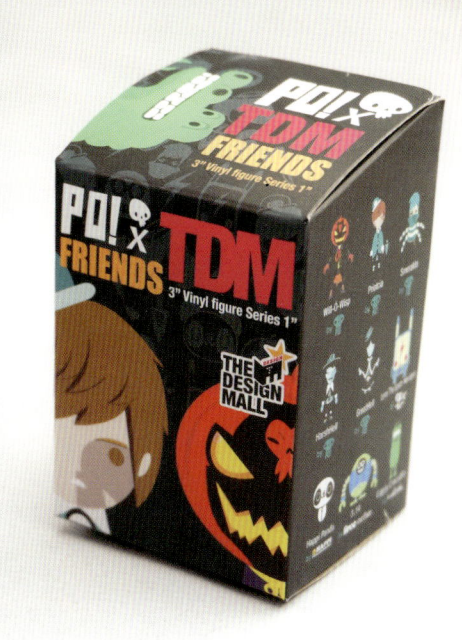

## CHAOS MONKEY

Design Agency: bunkadesign.com
Creative Director: bunka
Design Director: bunka
Designer: bunka
Country: France
Photographer: ARTOYZ

Title: chaos monkey serie X

■■■ CHAOS MONKEY

Designer: bunka

Title: RELEASE CHAOS MONKEY @ ARTOYZ GALLERY    Designer: bunka

## ▶■ RELEASE CHAOS MONKEY @ ARTOYZ GALLERY

Design Agency: bunkadesign.com
Creative Director: bunka
Design Director: bunka
Designer: bunka
Country: France
Photographer: 3D Gregos

Title: SNAFU
Designer: bunka

# SWEETIE

Design Agency: ARTOYZ
Creative Director: STÉPHANE LEVALLOIS
Design Director: STÉPHANE LEVALLOIS
Designer: STÉPHANE LEVALLOIS
Country: Singapore
Photographer: WALDO LEE

Title :BETTER - HELL 1-2
Designer: Yann Le Nevé

## CHAOS KONG

Design Agency: bunkadesign.com
Creative Director: bunka
Design Director: bunka
Designer: bunka
Country: France
Photographer: ARTOYZ

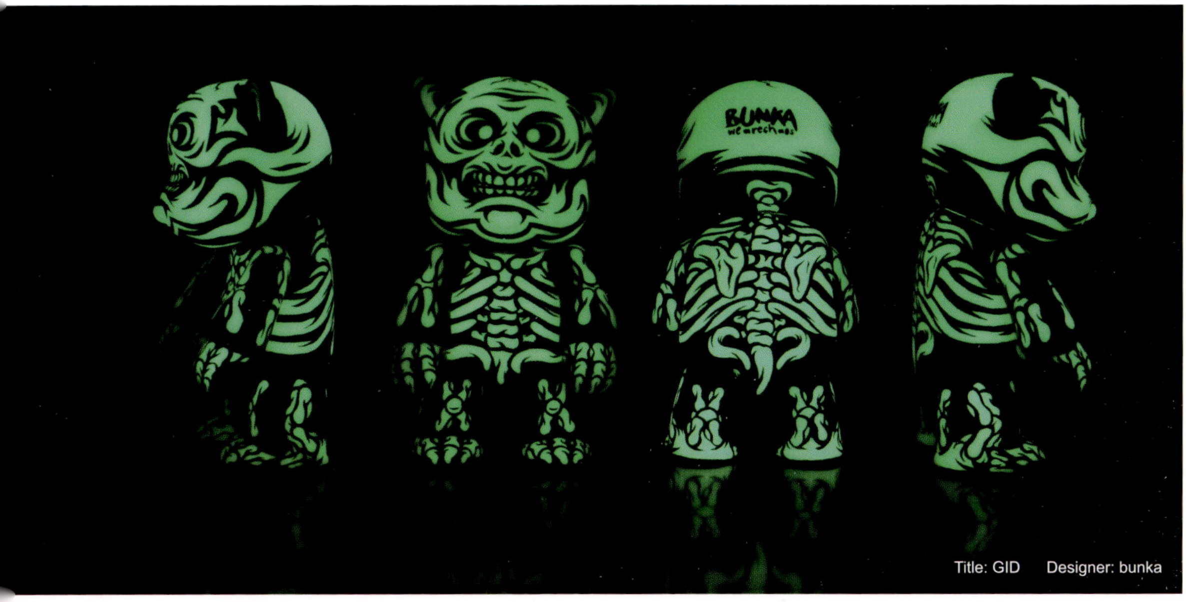

Title: GID    Designer: bunka

Title: CHAOS KONG    Designer: bunka

## CHAOS ELEMENT

Design Agency: bunkadesign.com
Creative Director: GREGOS
Design Director: GERGOS
Designer: bunka niark aisk gregos
Country: France
Photographer: 3D Gregos

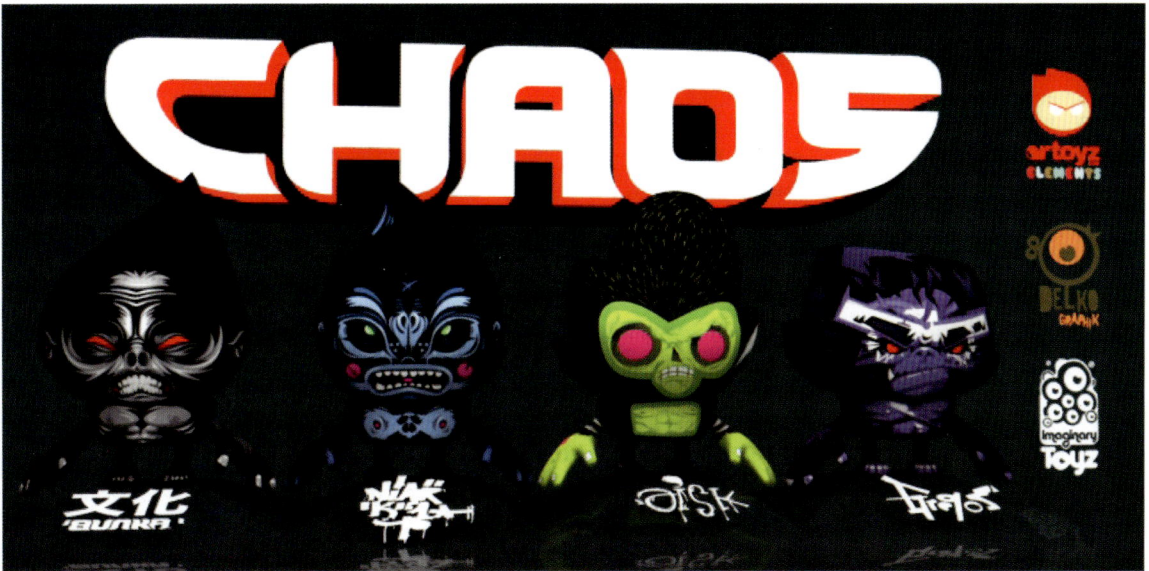

## CERRITO

This Art Toy figures represent the appearances of an Unidentified Mystic Animal called "Cerrito", which sudenly appears, smiles and later disappears again, producing an epiphany to the casual witness.
Hand painted, one of a kind resin pieces are part of a wide lineup of versions of Cerito appearances. Commonly used as Adoration Objects, Lucky Charms or Magnets for Mysterious Powers.

Design Agency: (freelance)
Creative Director: César Zanardi
Design Director: César Zanardi
Country: Argentina
Designer: César Zanardi
Photographer: César Zanardi and José Zanardi

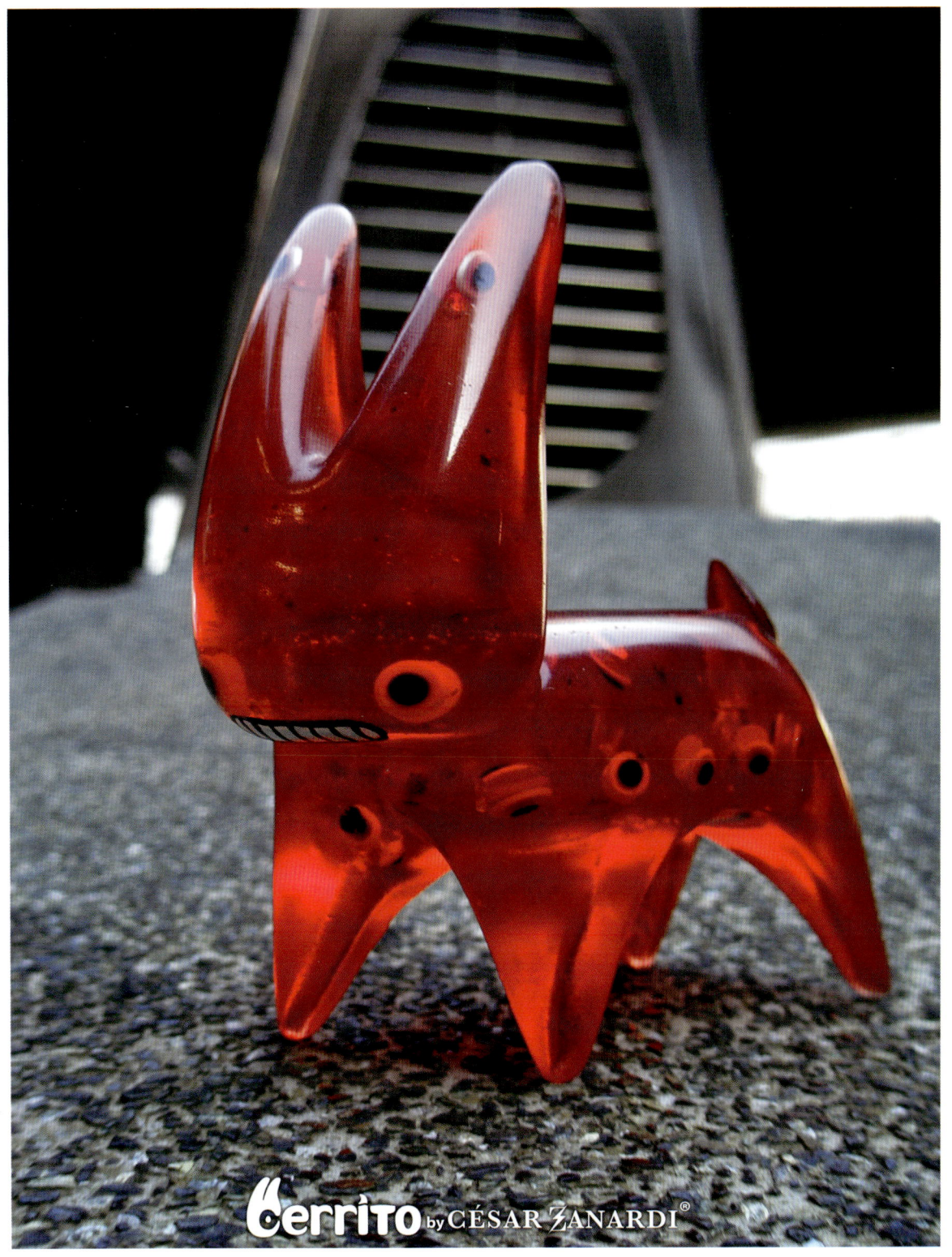

## Lofing & The Magical Mushroom

Lofing belongs to a group of creatures known as the Wackymons. They come from different places but united after their homeland was destroyed. Together, they created a new home called 'The Dreamland' and became good friends in the process. Lofing became their leader and would lead them through all kinds of difficulties. No matter how tough things are going, Lofing would always encourage them to stay optimistic.
Lofing is the main character and leader of Wackymons. Lofing is the largest of them all but is gentle and has a kind heart. Lofing is good spirited as well and serves as a positive influence for the rest of them.
"The Dreamland is a magical happy dreamland in my heart ." Said Shenly (Artist). The artworks combine' The Beauty of Parasite World' with her humorous sense of Character Design. Most of the artworks are influenced by the beauty of abstract parasitic life forms and the nature that surrounds us.

D'creativeaholic X Dweey is a collaboration between D'creativeaholic and Dweey. Dweey is a customisable toy which is generally a blank canvas for artists to exercise their creativity. This art piece by D'creativeholic draws from the artist's imagination and influence of the parasitic world.

Design Agency: D'creativeaholic & Dweey（Fusionwave Creative Consultancy）
Creative Director: Shenly Yee
Design Director: Shenly Yee
Country: Singapore
Designer: Shenly Yee
Photographer: Shenly Yee

## SAVE THE SEVEN SEAS MECHSKUHL MK1(RECON) SKUHL

Custom paint work on vinyl figures.
Design Agency: The Ink & Clog Studio
Greative Director: CLOGTWO
Design Director: Inkten
Country: Singapore
Designer: CLOGTWO
Photographer: Eman Raharno Jeman

## DANCING SKELETON
## C-BOMB HXCBOMB
## TRESPASSER BO55

Custom paint work on vinyl figures.
Designer: CLOGTWO

AIRBOURNE TROOPER
GALVXY
THE HIDDEN PEOPLE
LABBIT

Custom paint work on vinyl figures.
Designer: CLOGTWO

## 5 (L) / The Butcher (R)

Designer: Tomasz Płonka
Country: Poland
Client: Self initiated
Photographer: Tomasz Płonka(5)
vinylcanvas.com(The Butcher)

# Horse

Designer: Tomasz Płonka
Country: Poland
Client: Self initiated
Photographer: Tomasz Płonka

# Rabbies

## KANSHA-KUN

Crafted an image character of creative production GROUNDRIDDIM.
GROUNDRIDDIM is a crew of a creative agency formed by many talented musicians such as HIFANA, CHINZA DOPENESS, DJ UPPERCUT, and etc & Graphic Designers and Visual Producers / Directors.
"KANSHA" is a Japanese word means "RESPECT", so KANSHA-KUN is like a statue of respect.

Design Agency: GROUNDRIDDIM
Creative Director: TKO, YUYA(GROUNDRIDDIM)
Design Director: TKO, MAHARO(GROUNDRIDDIM)
Designer: TKO
Country: Japan
Photographer: TKO

Title: KZO machine!!

Title: TOKKOU-YAROU (B.A. & DMC VAN)

Title: HANABEAM

Title: CHIN-CHUCK

Title: DMC JPN DREAM TEAM

## SCOTT & RIVERS

Crafted the unit of Rivers Cuomo from U.S. rock band Weezer & Scott Murphy from ALLiSTER.

Designer: TKO

Title: THE NEXT MOVEMENT

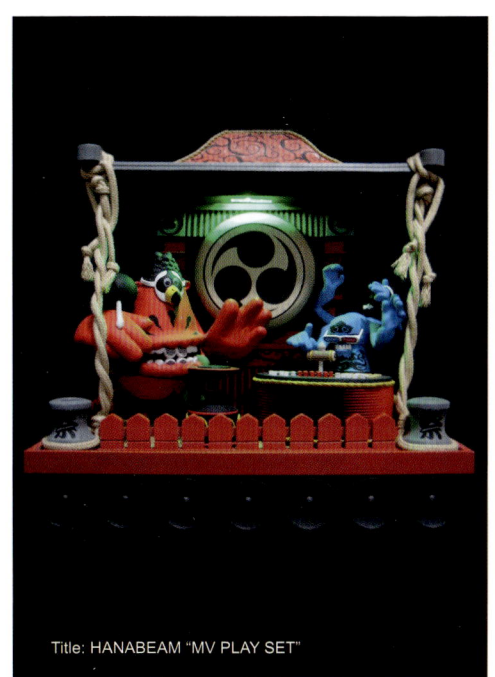

Title: HANABEAM "MV PLAY SET"

Title: ENTER THE WU-TANG

Title: MAGIC NUMBER

■ STITCH

Designer: VISEone
Country: Germany

315

# CAPTAIN AMERICA

Designer: VISEone

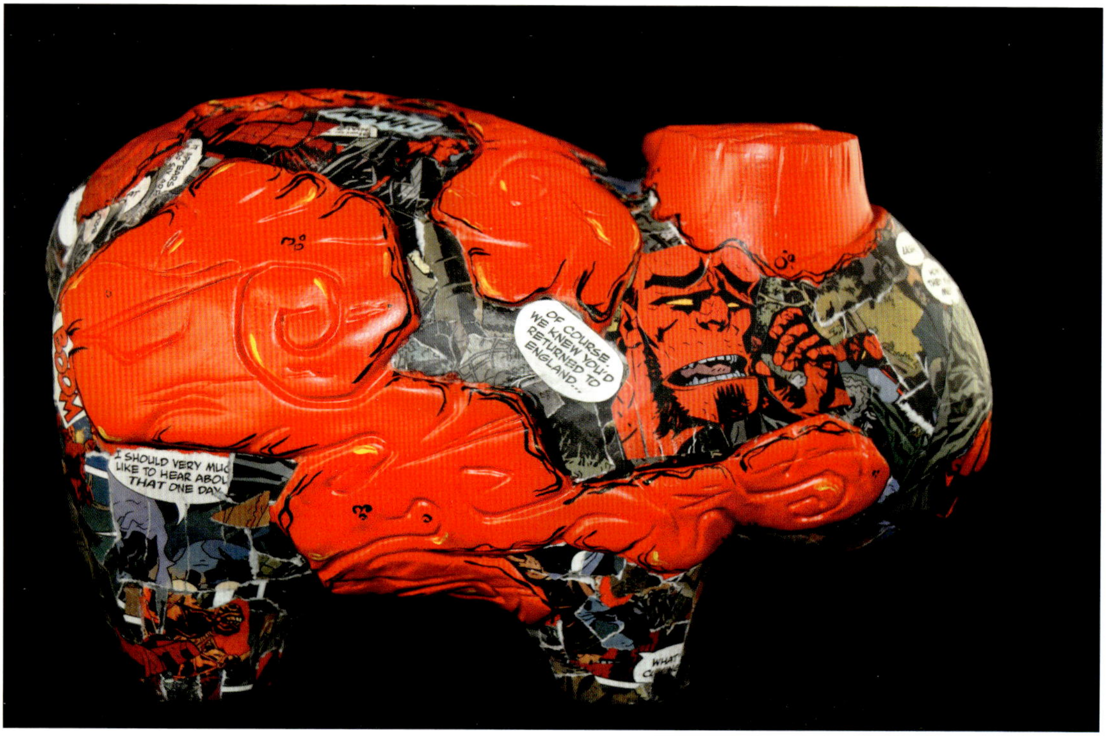

■ ■ ■ TORCH

Designer: VISEone

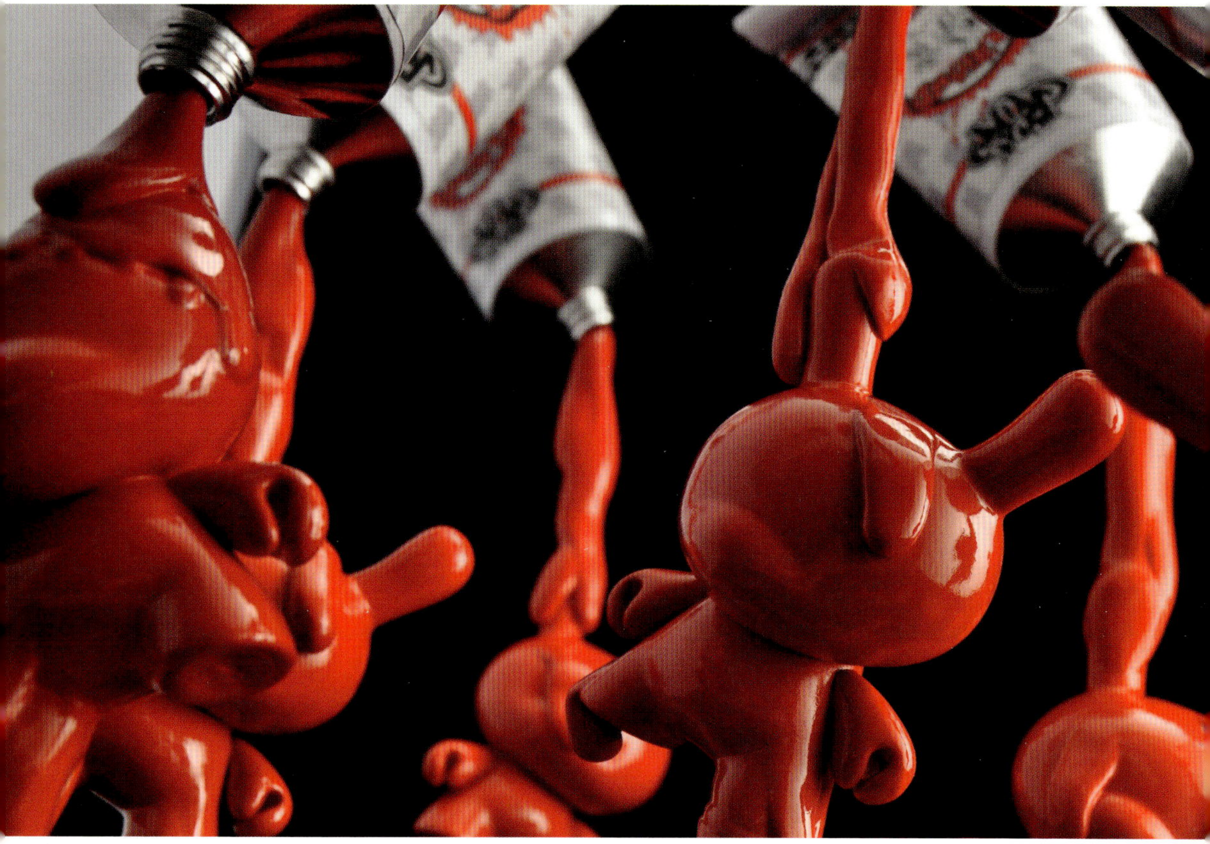

## RED TUBE DUNNYS

Designer: VISEone

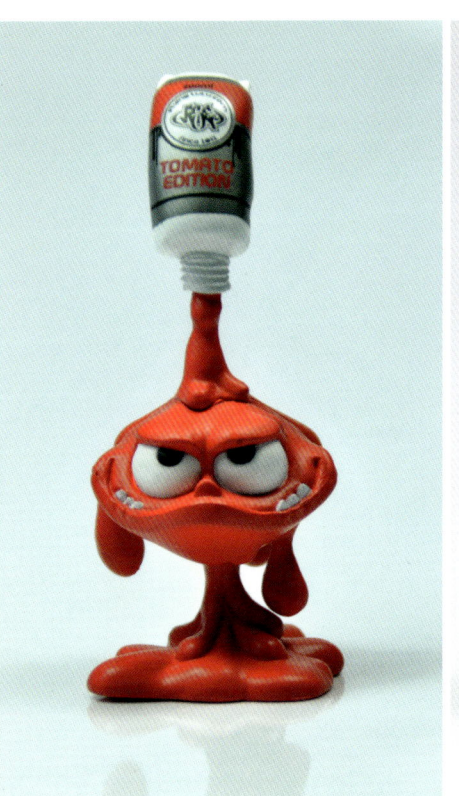

Designer: VISEone

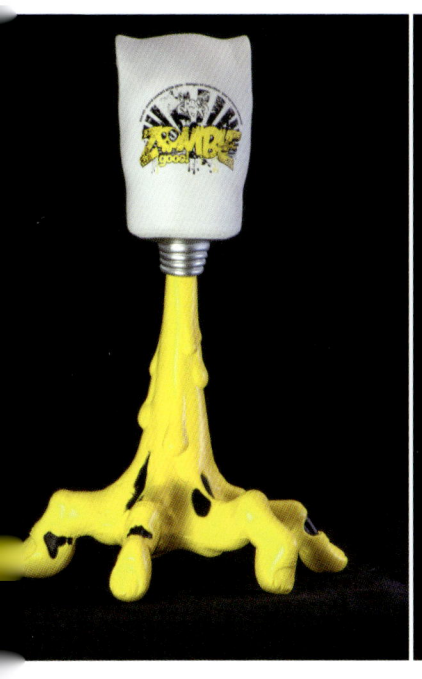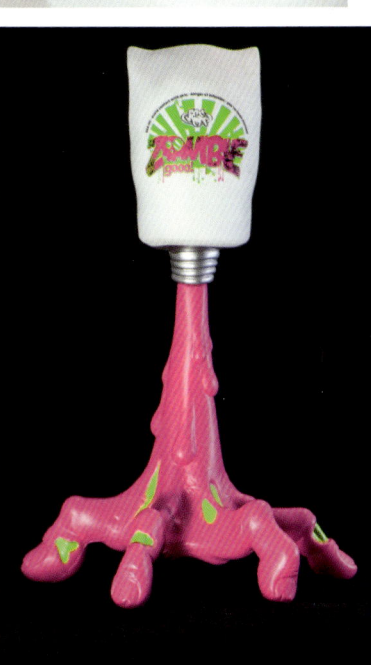

## Stitches and Glue

StitchesandGlue.com

Project QiQi was curated by Creo Design for the first ever UK ToyCon show which was held in London in April, 2013. Artists from all over the world were given the opportunity to showcase their unique talent and style on the lovely QiQi platform. With no set brief artists were allowed creative freedom to do whatever they wanted and the results are a mix of true artist style and imagination.

Creative Director: Goh Jit Hee (Ziqi), Chris Alexander (Creo Design)
Design Agency: Ziqi, Creo Design
Country:Singapore   Scotland,UK

Lisa Rae Hansen

ibreaktoys.com

**Akinori Oishi**

blog.aki-air.com
facebook.com/akinori.oishi.art

Zam Art

Uplife exhibition and fashion design.
Chocolate Rain x Sanrio upcycling fabric.

Creative Director: Ms Prudence Mak
Design Director: Ms Prudence Mak
Designer: CO1 Design School Students
Country: Hong Kong, China
Photographer: CO1 Design School Students

EAT & PLAY, by Chocolate Rain

## EAT & PLAY, by Chocolate Rain

Eat & Play is a combination of pure passion, commitment, believe, hard work, created by Prudence Mak, Chefo, and her team of young talents of Chocolate Rain. It will give u a delicious and joyful multi sensory experience. We welcome who would like to explore something totally new and forward thinking in our city. In E&P you will find, colorful smile, a 100% unique handmade interior where you will have a sweet and full of WOOOOWWWWW moments in the dining experience.

We prepare for you daily (made in the kitchen of Tuen), special dessert (our base concept)Hey, this are not the dessert you think about, they are super different, in texture, combinations, story, presentation and of course in taste. Nothing in E&P will be boring or done already, you will have to be open to experiments with us and have lot of fun, trust us, because we will only care to do our best for you, give to you something to remember. We will also serve savory, snack such as the EAT set menu or PLAY surprise menu (and much more…) base of the season to let you have a good dinner. E&P is a wonderland where u will feel happy and fresh from a long or stress day of work, where you feel at home, with respect, creative and caring. We make you became part of our dreams.

Design Agency: Chocolate Rain Jewelery & Design Co. Ltd
Creative Director: Ms Prudence Mak
Design Director: Ms Prudence Mak
Country: Hong Kong, China
Photographer: Mr Daniel Cheng

335

## Kawaii Charuca

Charuca characters illustration.

Creative Director: Charuca
Design Director: Charuca
Country: Spain
Designer: Charuca

**Kawaii is all about Sugar!**

## Charuca Minitoys

Charuca characters vinyl figures.

Creative Director: Charuca
Design Director: Charuca
Country: Spain
Designer: Charuca
Client: Comansi
Photographer: Rosario Vargas

## Charuca Kawaii Plushes

Carmi, Rosita Sugar and Alin plush toys.

Creative Director: Charuca
Design Director: Charuca
Country: Spain
Designer: Charuca
Client: Famosa
Photographer: Rosario Vargas

Husky x3

Husky x3

Husky x3

357

## Husky x3

## Husky x3

■■ Husky x3

Husky x3

■■■ Apexlife concept shop opening special vinyl figure

Designer: Winson Ma

Title: Handmade version vinyl figure   Designer: Winson Ma   Country: Hong Kong, China

Apexlife concept shop opening special vinyl figure

Apexplorers character "Otto"

Designer: Winson Ma

Title: Apexworkbot characters    Designer: Winson Ma

# First creation of Winson action figure " Space Adam"

Designer: Winson Ma
Country: Hong Kong, China

## 13 ART

Designer: 13

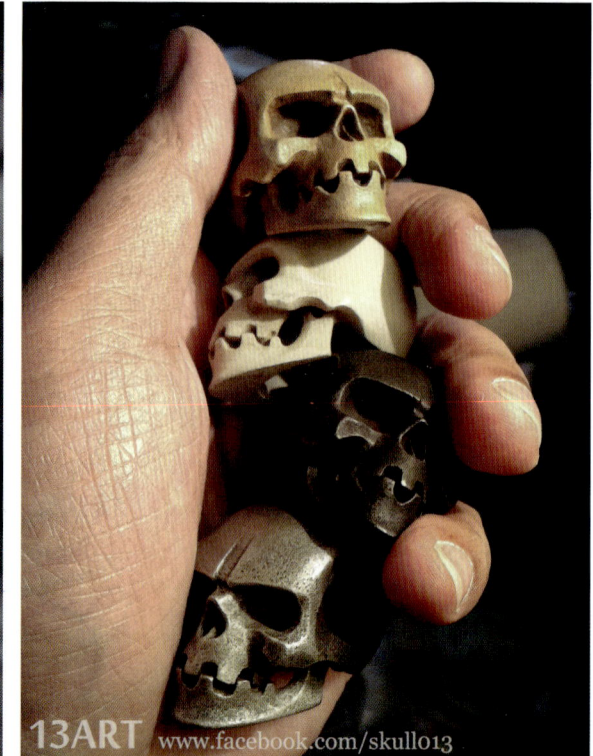

Designer: 13

## 13 ART

Designer: 13

# Designer Toys

Designer: Bowo Baghaskara

## AlterEGO_Sandman

Country: Germany
Designer: dust | David Stegmann
Photographer: dust | David Stegmann
Material: Polyurethane (Plastic)
Height: 7.5cm
Limited to 10 pieces

Title: AlterEGO_Guard

# R.B.S. IV - open helmet

Designer: dust | David Stegmann
Photographer: dust | David Stegmann
Material: Polyurethane (Plastic)
Height: 6.5cm
Limited to 10 pieces

## RAS2010_regular | RAS2010_greyguard

Designer: dust | David Stegmann
Photographer: dust | David Stegmann
Material: Polyurethane (Plastic)
Height: 7.5cm
Limited to 40 pieces(RAS2010_regular )
unique pice(RAS2010_greyguard)

## RAS_regular

Designer: dust | David Stegmann
Photographer: dust | David Stegmann
Material: Polyurethane (Plastic)
Height: 7.5cm
Limited to 50 pieces

### Hell Lotus Master Teddy San

Country: Germany
Designer: dust | David Stegmann
Photographer: dust | David Stegmann
Material: Epoxy, viny
Height: 20cm

## Teddy Assault Tank

Designer: dust | David Stegmann
Photographer: dust | David Stegmann
Material: Epoxy, vinyl
Height: 7.5cm

# Teddytank HXW7

Designer: dust | David Stegmann
Photographer: dust | David Stegmann
Height: 18cm

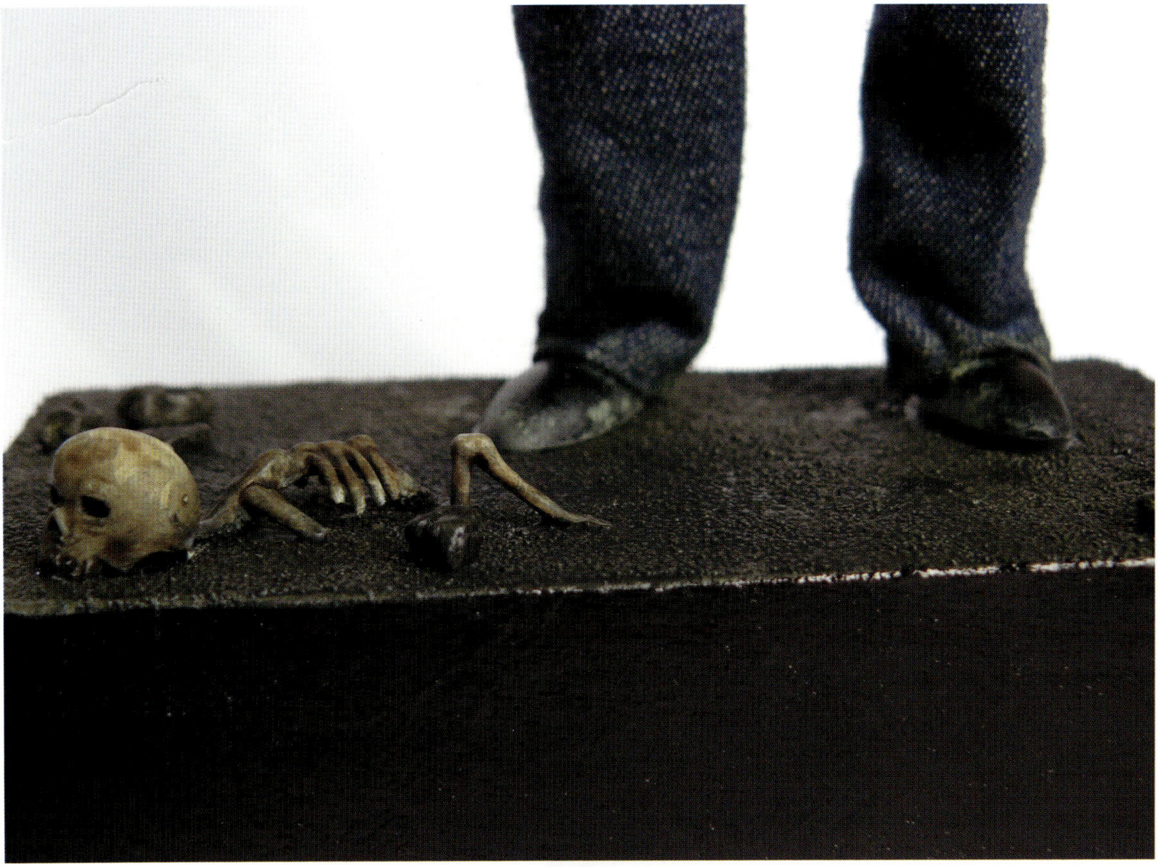

## RAS 69th Ground Defense

Designer: dust | David Stegmann
Photographer: dust | David Stegmann
Material: Epoxy, plastic

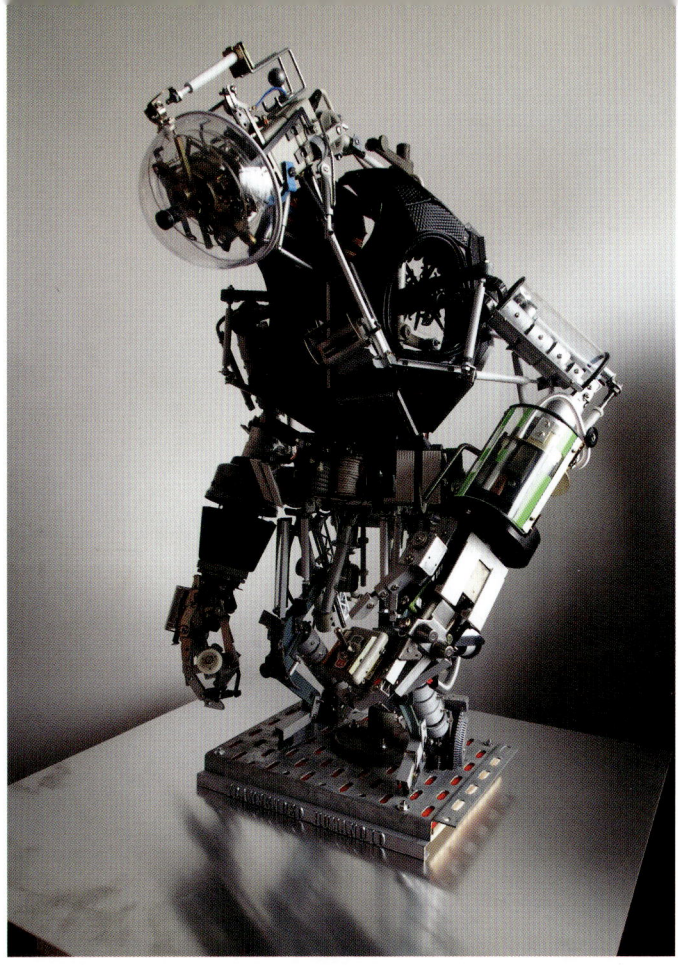
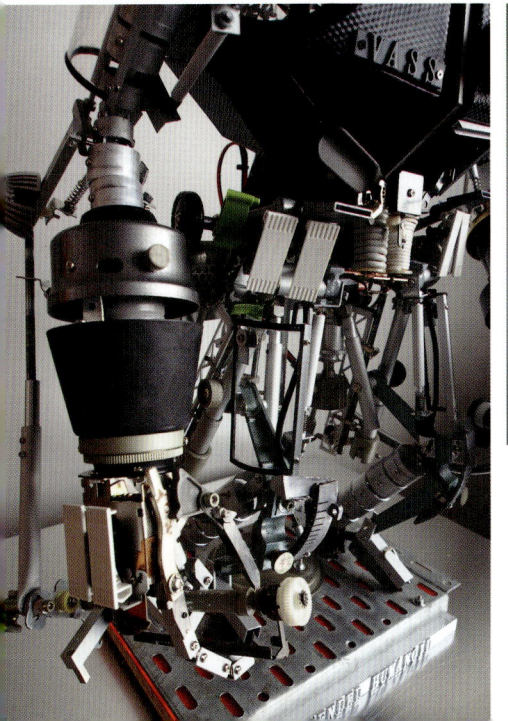

This scenario triggers an aggressive accumulation of virtual assets. DMVs start attacking each other to seize control over resources. Cybercrime intensifies, but authorities' action is completely compromised due to their obsolete systems.

To counter such anarchic environment in the cyber space, the VASS+ program is initiated for assets protection, these neurorobotic suits are widely used for anti-theft, virtual resources administration and hosts' sustainability.

# SUPER PLAYER

Editor-in-chief: Y&Y(Yang Liu&Jianing Yuan)
Editor: Nan Xia
Proofreader: Nan Xia
Art Director: Yannick(Jianing Yuan)
Design Director: Yang Liu
Printing Specialist: Yang Liu
Design and Layout: Nan Xia, Yang Liu

Publisher: DESIGNERBOOKS
Unit D, 16/F, Cheuk Nang 21st Century Plaza, 250 Hennessy Road,
Wanchai, Hong Kong
Tel: +852-2575-5186
Fax: +852-2891-1996
E-mail: edit@designerbooks.com.cn

Distributor: DESIGNERBOOKS
A108,Kelin Creative plaza, 107#, North Street, Dongsi, Dongcheng District, Beijing, China
Tel: 0086-10-6400-3080 (Beijing)
　　 0086-21-5596-7639 (Shanghai)
　　 0086-755-8825-0425 (Shenzhen)
　　 0086-20-8756-5010 (Guangzhou)
　　 0086-28-6465-8008 (Chengdu)
　　 0086-27-6566-2067 (Wuhan)
Fax: 0086-10-64018430-822
E-mail: import01@designerbooks.com.cn
http: //www.designerbooks.com.cn

Printed in China

All rights reserved. No part of this publication may be reproduced in any form or by any means, graphic, electronic or mechanical, including photocopying and recording by an information storage and retrieval system without permission in writing from the publisher.

ISBN: 978-988-12232-0-3
© Copyright 2015

## Teddytank HXW7

Designer: dust | David Stegmann

# Deamons of the Future - Stormtrooper Hunter TypeA

Designer: dust | David Stegmann
Photographer: dust | David Stegmann
Height: 33cm

## RAS 69th Ground Defense

Designer: dust | David Stegmann

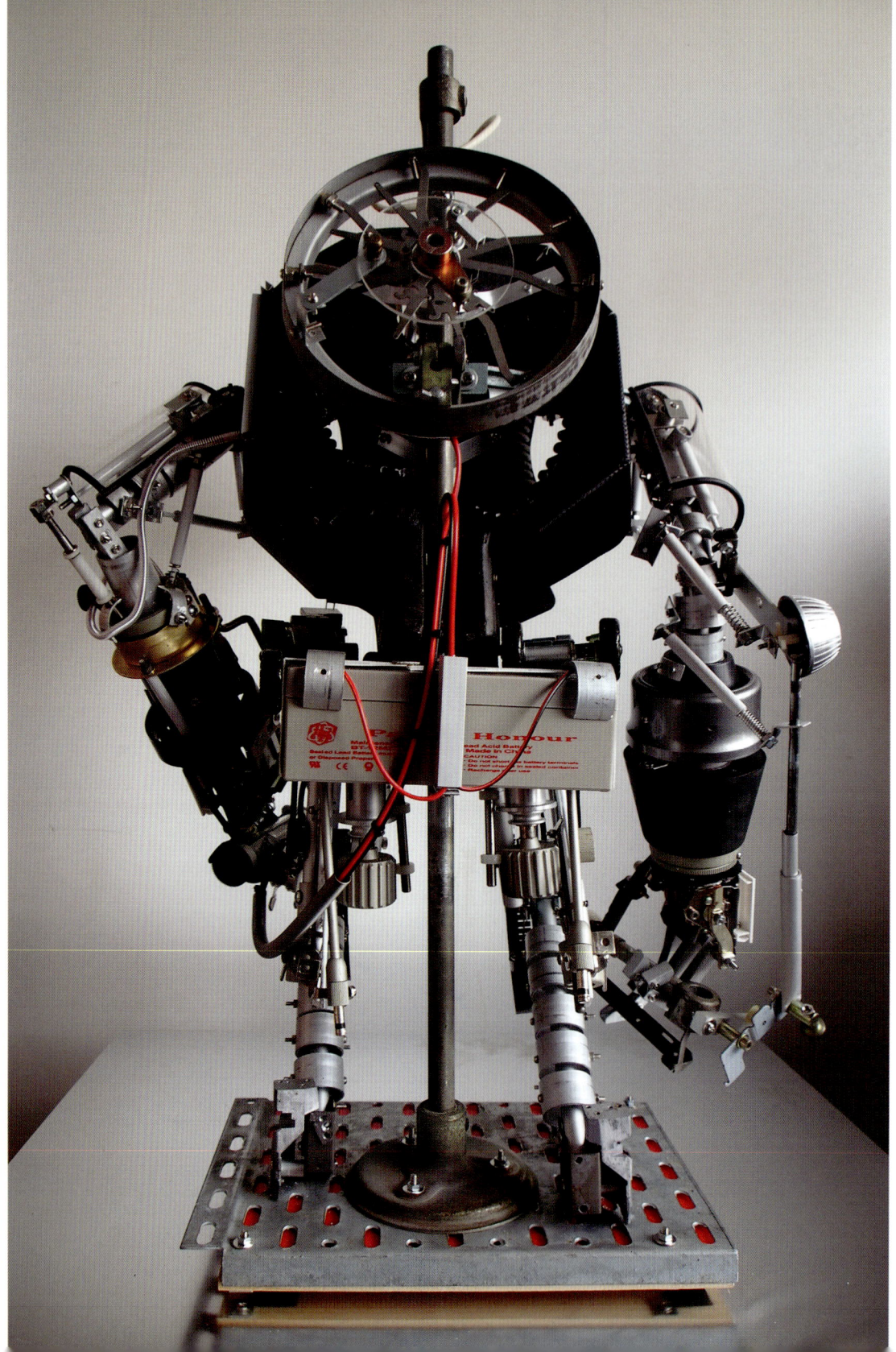

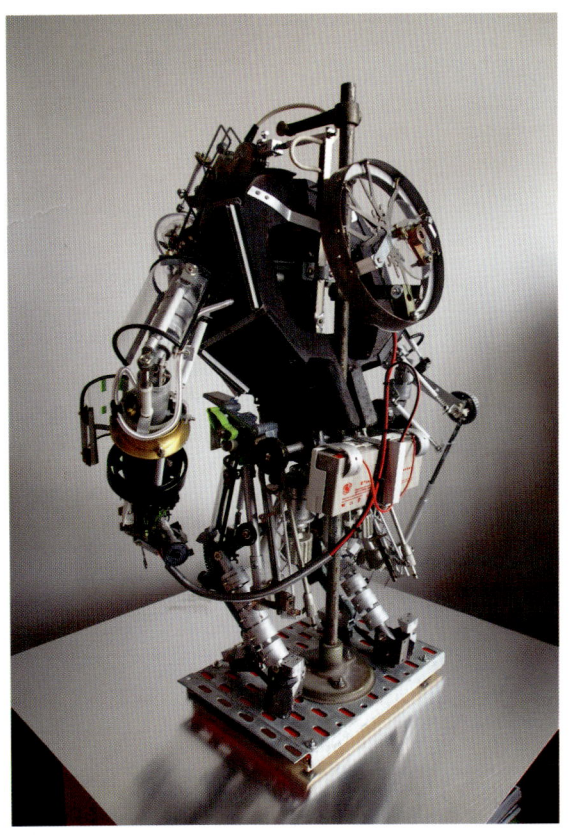
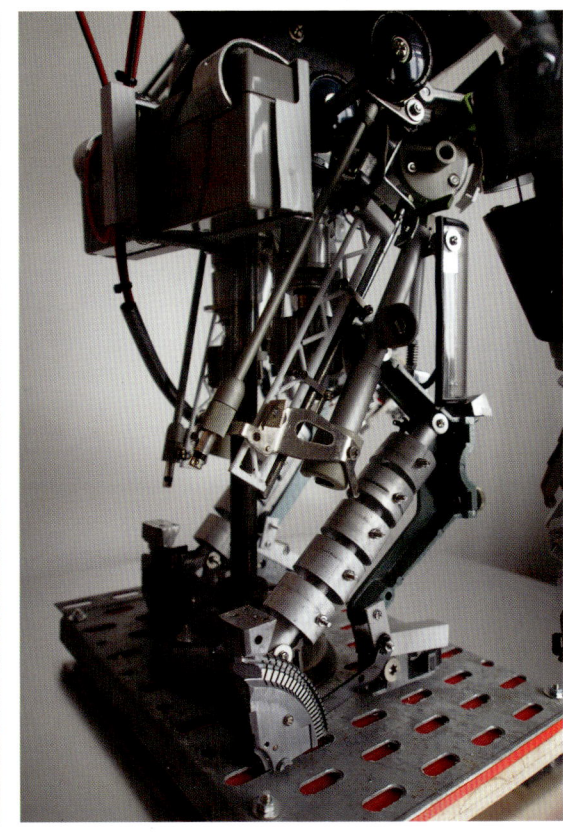

## ▎▎▎ VASS+Transcended Humanoid

Design Agency: Personal Work
Creative Director: n/a
Design Director: n/a
Country: Hong Kong, China
Designer: Aaron Liu
Photographer: Aaron Liu
Height: 780mm
Material: Metal / Acrylic/ Mixed Media
Synopsis: "VASS+"- Virtual Assets Sustainable Suits

In the near future, under the phenomenon of "Global Neuro Linkage Syndrome", human brains are on-line 24-7. As long as human conscious remain active in the network, death is only justified as a biological failure. This population group is classified as DMV – Dead Mind Vessels.

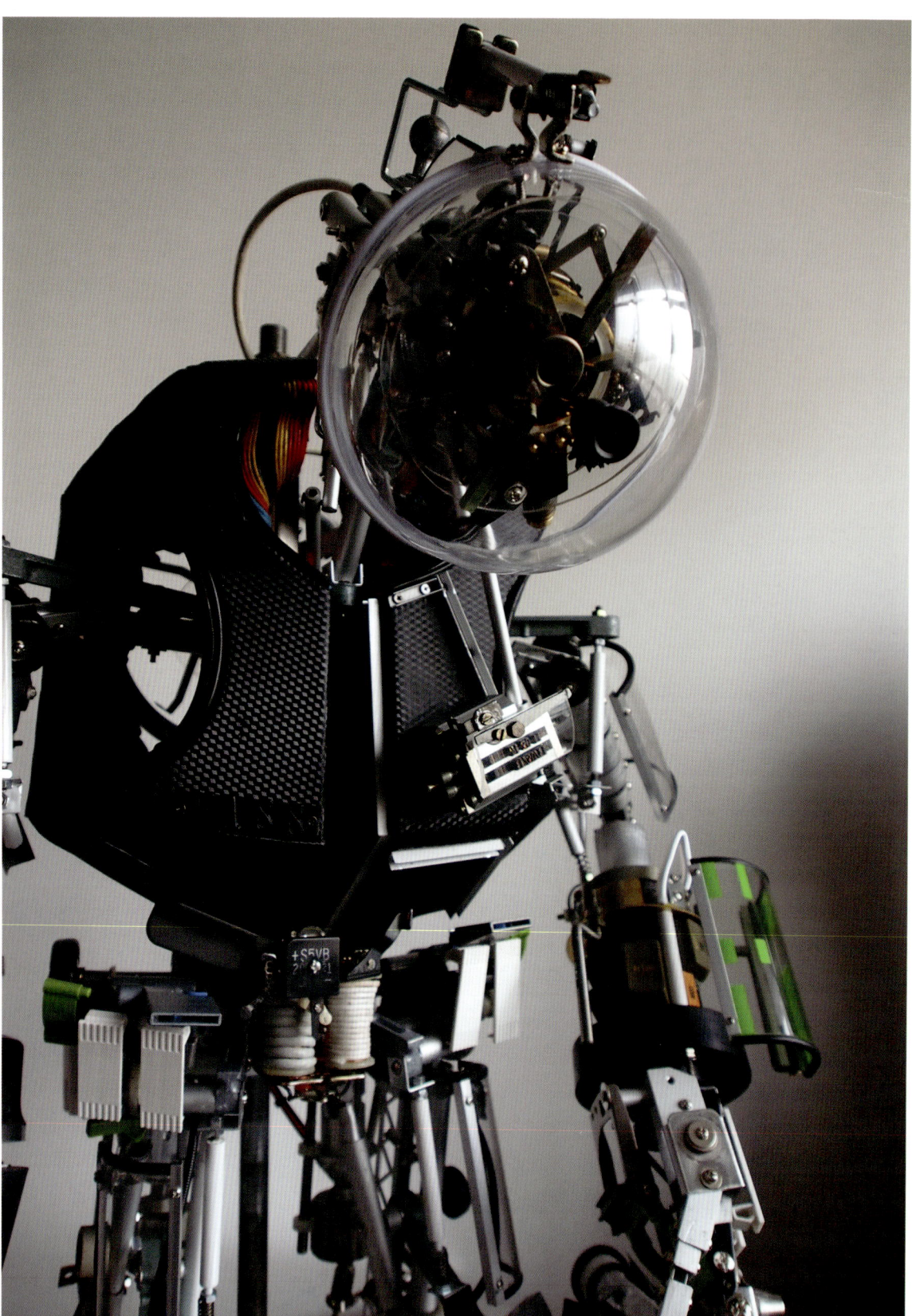

## XW7 Munny

Designer: dust | David Stegmann
Photographer: dust | David Stegmann
Material: Epoxy and vinyl
Height: 26cm